Michael: For my parents, Bill and Greta,
for all they have done. And for my past, current,
and future colleagues at Reputation.com for
changing the course of the Internet for the better.

David: For Steph, Cooper, and Riley
for being amazing and supportive.

THE
REPUTATION
ECONOMY

CROWN BUSINESS is a trademark and CROWN and the Rising Sun colophon
are registered trademarks of Random House LLC.

Crown Business books are available at special discounts for bulk purchases for
sales promotions or corporate use. Special editions, including personalized
covers, excerpts of existing books, or books with corporate logos, can be created
in large quantities for special needs. For more information, contact Premium
Sales at (212) 572-2232 or e-mail specialmarkets@randomhouse.com.

Library of Congress Cataloging-in-Publication Data is available upon request.

ISBN 978-0-385-34759-4
eBook ISBN 978-0-385-34760-0

PRINTED IN THE UNITED STATES OF AMERICA

Book design by Ralph Fowler / rlfdesign
Jacket design by Gabriel Levine
Jacket art: Shutterstock/A-R-T

10 9 8 7 6 5 4 3 2 1

First Edition

THE
REPUTATION
ECONOMY

How to Optimize
Your Digital Footprint in a
World Where Your Reputation
Is Your Most Valuable Asset

MICHAEL FERTIK
AND DAVID C. THOMPSON

CROWN
BUSINESS

New York

Contents

THE
REPUTATION
ECONOMY

1

Welcome to the Reputation Economy

REPUTATION IS POWER.

Your reputation defines who will talk to you and what they will do with you or for you. It determines whether your bank will lend you money to buy a house or a car; it determines whether your landlord will accept you as a tenant; it determines which employers will hire you or whether you can even get a job at all; it may determine the types of special offers and VIP experiences you receive; and it can even profoundly affect your dating prospects. Your reputation among insurers determines your ability to get coverage for your health, auto, home, or life. And your reputation with the government can even determine whether you are investigated for a crime.

And it's getting more powerful than ever. Thanks to rapid advances in digital technology, your reputation will become ubiquitous, permanent, and available worldwide—whether you like it or not. Everywhere you go, other people will be able to instantly access information about your reputation—with or without your knowledge or consent.

This goes well beyond so-called Big Data, the trend of huge amounts of data being collected and stored. Instead, the new Reputation Economy depends on what we'll call Big Analysis— the power of new systems to extract personal predictions from these massive collections of data and turn them into action: denying you a loan; getting you an interview for a job that wasn't even advertised; or even turning a potential date away at the door. All of this based on your reputation—newly digitized and networked, in all kinds of dizzyingly sophisticated ways.

Of course, reputation has always been important. Just ask anyone who has ever lived in a small town about how long a reputation can last and how it can color your interactions— especially if you ever make a big mistake. But back before the Reputation Economy, reputation was earned slowly among peers and dissipated over time: very few people knew anything about most non-celebrities, and a reputation lasted only as long as a human memory.

Today, digital technology has made it possible to collect, store, analyze, and distribute all kinds of information about you, ranging from your demographic profile to your driving record to a complete list of all your online activities. This so-called data mining—the 2010s buzzword for the trend toward collecting huge amounts of data about nearly every subject imaginable— exists because technology has made it nearly costless to collect and store data. The easiest way to understand the capacity of digital data storage today is that a 1-terabyte disk drive holds more information than is housed in an average research library. Such drives are readily available to consumers, fit neatly in a large pants pocket or a small purse, and cost comfortably less than $100—and the price is falling lower every year. The result is that today a company or an individual doesn't have to have the resources of a giant corporation (or the National Security Agency) to store a seemingly infinite amount of personal information about other individuals. This collapse in the price of storage (which can be neatly traced across thousands of years from the painstaking process of copying clay tablets through the printing press through magnetic media of today and the massive solid-state devices of the near future) allows nearly unlimited data to be stored and processed in a way that was never previously possible.

Now that digital data storage is practically free, everything that can be will be collected and stored—permanently. In fact, it is fast becoming cheaper to keep large data sets than to try to figure out which data to delete. And once the data is available, you can bet somebody will find a use for it. As a result, massive digital dossiers are being developed on every individual, right down to the websites you visit and the links you click on. There is even a fast-growing underground economy of archives and data storage sites that quietly collect records of trillions of online activities, often just waiting for someone to figure out a way to make use of all that data.

But while Big Data is scary to think about, this data in and of itself is worth nothing—it's just a series of 1s and 0s—if companies don't know how to use it. The real power (for both good and evil) of Big Data comes in the next step: unlocking actionable intelligence through new computer systems and algorithms that sort and sift through millions of data points to find meaning. Which is why the future will be dominated not by those companies and individuals who collect the most data but by those who can make the most sense of these massive data sets—Big Analysis. If Big Data is knowing that you're sitting on a gold mine, Big Analysis is actually getting it out of the ground and turning it into bullion.

The change from Big Data to Big Analysis is huge. It's not just that our storage capacity has grown. Our ability to parse, sort, and analyze that data has increased exponentially as well. If Moore's Law—a general rule that computers get about twice as powerful every two years—continues to hold true, as it has for decades, then the power of digital analysis will continue to grow. As a result, people are beginning to entrust more and more decisions to computers, including millions of decisions formerly made by humans.

To see how this will affect *you*, think about how companies are already developing systems to make millions of decisions about consumers (like you) each minute. And the scope of these decisions is quickly expanding from reasonably unsurprising ones (like trying to reduce credit card fraud by identifying unusual transactions) to ones that would shock you: ranging from insurers denying coverage on the basis of online activity, through employers automatically deciding whom to hire and promote on the basis of computer-driven analysis, to mobile phone applications that allow instant background checks at bars. What decisions will be made on the basis of the fact that you purchased this book? Hopefully good ones, but we'll spend the next chapters exploring them.

Soon, companies will even be using the massive data sets they have acquired to assign you reputation scores—similar to a FICO credit score—based on your reputation for everything from hard work to financial responsibility to health. Just as search engines allow users to search the Web for information, "reputation engines" will allow companies—and, increasingly, everyday people—to search your digital footprints for information about all your online *and offline* activities and interactions. Think of your credit score as a very primitive version of what we will see in the coming Reputation Economy; if your credit score is like a traditional landline telephone handset, then future reputation scores will be like the newest iPhone. This will happen whether or not you want to participate, and these scores will be used by others to make major decisions about your life, such as whether to hire, insure, or even date you.

These decisions and others are happening faster than ever before. Forget what you've heard about making decisions in the blink of an eye; today, major decisions are being made by computers thousands of times faster. A human blink can take up to four hundred milliseconds; in that time, an average laptop computer can perform almost one *billion* calculations. The impact of this increasing speed is huge; in fact, these reputation engines—powered by dizzyingly sophisticated algorithms—are already picking over millions of records per second to identify good and bad credit risks, employees who might be considering quitting, and more. Take an easy example: Have you started browsing LinkedIn at work more than usual? Many algorithms view that as a big red flag for employees looking for a new job— for better or worse. If it's caught by a recruiter, look forward to increased cold calls trying to lure you into new jobs. If it's caught by your company, look forward to either a conversation about what it would take to keep you—or a swift kick toward the door.

Not surprisingly, companies have already sprung up to supply this data to anyone willing to pay cash for it. Sellers range from wholesalers like Intelius, which sells millions of records at a time, to retailers like Spokeo.com that allow consumers to pay a few dollars to find anyone's home address. But the real value won't be for the companies who sell the data wholesale; it will be for those companies who are best able to use it to predict behavior. For example, when Google launched, it didn't have the largest index of Web pages or the most comprehensive directory, but it leaped ahead of competitors because it was the best at identifying relevant search results from a smaller set of data. The same goes for whatever company will be the Google of personal information. Indeed, this is a holy grail so valuable that in 2011 venture capital firms invested $2.47 billion (yes, *billion*) into launching companies that manipulate, process, store, or sell large data sets—often about consumers.[1] This number increased to at least $3.6 billion in 2013.[2]

Reputation is equally powerful for businesses, professionals, and private individuals. In business, up to 75 percent of a company's value in the market is its reputation;[3] in your personal life, the figure for reputation may be closer to 100 percent. In fact, because of the growth of digital reputation, your reputation may be more valuable than cash currency, as Cory Doctorow, bestselling sci-fi author, described in *Down and Out in the Magic Kingdom,* where the "Whuffie," a fictional reputation currency, came to replace money. In Doctorow's words, "Whuffie recaptured the true essence of money: in the old days, if you were broke but respected, you wouldn't starve; contrariwise, if you were rich and hated, no sum could buy you security and peace. By measuring the thing that money really represented— your personal capital with your friends and neighbors—you more accurately gauged your success."[4] Sadly, this is not as far-fetched as it sounds; in our new digital age, our own version of the Whuffie is rapidly becoming a reality.

This book is about how to become "reputation rich" in a world where reputation is becoming more valuable than money or power.

Building the "Economy" in the Reputation Economy

The "Reputation Economy" is how we describe this world where reputation is instantly analyzed, stored, and used as your passport to special treatment and benefits. In the Reputation Economy, you will be able to use your reputation like cash, putting it up as collateral to secure your debts and to make transactions you could never otherwise make.

This new digital reputation will touch all aspects of your life. Imagine walking into a hotel for the first time and being immediately greeted by a well-dressed concierge, who ushers you past the regular line and directly to a VIP check-in station. He offers you a cold drink while the desk clerk prepares your room keys. As you sip, the desk clerk asks if you'd like a complimentary upgrade to a corner room with a city view. Of course, you accept, but you have one question: "Why me?" The clerk explains that his computer noticed that on the basis of your online comments and your travel history, you have very high scores for brand loyalty and social sharing—and that on the basis of your dedication to hard work, his computer expects you to continue to be well off for a number of years. He explains that the hotel would love to have your business in the future and that his computer calculated that giving you upgraded service could be enough to gain your business for life. When you booked your reservation, all of this was calculated automatically, transmitted wirelessly to the front desk, and used without your knowledge or consent.

Of course, your digital reputation will lead to more than just special hotel upgrades. The effect will be profound: with a good digital reputation you will be given special offers in all areas of your life, perhaps without even knowing why (and sometimes without even knowing that they are special offers); with a poor reputation, you will miss opportunities and never know what you're missing.

Not only that, but savvy individuals will use the power of reputation to turn traditional relationships on their heads. Applying for jobs the old-fashioned way is, well, old-fashioned: in the Reputation Economy, if you carefully craft a reputation for high-quality work, employers will find *you* and offer you the best jobs without your ever having to submit a job application. If you're single and have a positive reputation for romance (and maybe income, intelligence, and other positive qualities), the best dates will come to you without your having to spend hours on dating sites, deal with the "meat market" bar scene, or spend hours cruising phone dating apps. With a good reputation for finance, don't worry about calling payday lenders or bank after bank to try to get a loan: you will be entrusted to borrow money without traditional collateral, given express treatment at your bank, and given special rates with just your signature.

Of course, for every person who gets treated as a hotel VIP, there is somebody who is silently denied an opportunity without even knowing it. For every person given a chance of a lifetime at a dream job, there is somebody else who never got a callback because of a long-past mistake. And for every person who is given a special offer from a national bank, somebody else is subtly directed toward check cashing and other subprime finance.

The growth of the Reputation Economy has accelerated to multibillion-dollar levels not just because reputation is currency in its own right but also because there is also almost unlimited value to knowing other people's reputation to a level of detail that would have been shocking just a generation ago. In other words, your own reputation has value not just to you but to anyone who has dealings with you. For example, a health insurer would pay good money to identify risky clients, and a landlord (and neighbors) would happily spend large sums to identify (and blacklist) noisy would-be tenants before they can even submit an application. Consumers are already paying money for on-the-go reputation systems that they can run on their iPhone or Blackberry; one even allows daters to run criminal background checks on people they meet at bars (real tagline: "Look up before you hook up").

Professionals who have excellent digital reputations— reputations that are discoverable on and through the Internet— will get more inbound job offers than ones who don't. For example, professional programmers are already being judged by their "reputation score" through sites like Stack Overflow and Coderwall. Coderwall wants to expand automated scoring to cover programmers' "achievements" across many sites and even presents a "leaderboard" listing of those whom it perceives to be the best programmers. Similar services like Klout purport to identify the most influential and respected users of sites like Twitter, and "Klout scores" have already appeared on résumés as supposed proof of applicants' online reputation.

It's not just technology start-ups who are using data in this way. Insurance companies have publicly admitted that they use Facebook data to investigate claims,[5] and they have quietly initiated test projects using online data to rate potential policyholders on the basis of their online activity before giving a quote.[6] A leading journal for insurers has even proposed that insurers could look at data concerning the types of ads you click on to identify risks—if other people who click on similar ads are poor risks, you will be judged a poor risk as well.[7] Credit limits for charge cards are already being reduced without warning on the basis of predictions from spending patterns,[8] and from there it's a small step toward incorporating online activity into dynamic credit reductions: as one scholar wrote, "If guitar players or divorcing couples are more likely to renege on their credit-card bills, then the fact that you've looked at guitar ads or sent an e-mail to a divorce lawyer might cause a data aggregator to classify you as less credit-worthy."[9]

In fact, both Visa and MasterCard have started pilot programs to analyze consumers' transaction trends in order to better target advertisements. According to one report, "A holy grail would be to show, for instance, a weight-loss ad to a person who just swiped their card at a fast-food chain—then track whether that person bought the advertised products."[10] And perhaps less surprisingly, Vegas casinos are setting up interactive displays that target custom advertisements based on what their reputation engines know about the person walking by.[11]

To understand how this all works, suppose that late one night you happen to be up surfing the Internet and see a Web banner advertisement that promises, "Secret plant extract shreds 15 pounds in one week"—complete with a "before" stick figure with a potbelly and an "after" stick figure that is, well, stick-thin. Out of curiosity, you click on the ad.

In the world of Big Data, you've just sentenced yourself to weeks of banner advertisements promising weight loss: by clicking on the ad, you have ensured that your Web browser will be identified with weight-loss advertisements so that now, on every site you visit, you'll be greeted by banners proclaiming, "Secret trick to lose the love handles," "Amazing Aztec weight loss secret," "What the fat industry doesn't want you to know," and more. And the company that produces the ads will be using the data from you and thousands of other people to fine-tune the advertisements: Do more people click on the ad with the stick-figure "before" and "after" or on an ad with a photo of a glamorous and skinny model? Do more people click in the middle of the day or late at night? Which landing-page copy produces the most purchases? In the world of Big Data, the company behind the advertisements might even run tests on hundreds of computer-generated variants of its advertisements to see what features lead to the most clicks and the most purchases,

In the new world of Big Analysis things go a lot further. In the Reputation Economy, not only will you see more annoying advertisements for weight-loss products, but your click on the advertisement will affect your reputation scores on a multitude of dimensions. For clicking, whether out of intent to buy, morbid curiosity, or the slip of your wrist, on an advertisement that makes flagrantly unrealistic claims (sorry, but no plant extract can safely remove fifteen pounds in a week), you'll gain a score for being susceptible to advertising—or even just plain gullible. For being up late at night surfing the Web in the first place you may gain a score for insomnia and in turn poor physical or mental health—which may be negated and replaced with a "hardworking" score if the computer has reason to believe you're surfing for work-related reasons. And, for obvious reasons, the reputation engines will assume you have a serious weight problem—and your health scores could plummet (or, depending on the algorithm, your "self-improvement" score might even get a slight boost based on the fact that you were earnestly trying to improve your image, even if the purchase was unlikely to work).

But the impact of these scores goes a lot further than which ads follow you around the Internet. In the world of Big Data, only the company serving up the ads knows you're in the market for weight-loss products; in the Reputation Economy, so will any other company or individual who bothers to search for the information. There will be an impact on your financial standing: good luck getting a low-interest-rate loan if the bank knows that in addition to living at the edge of your means, you have a predilection for late-night purchases. Good luck with your romantic prospects (overweight? poor self-esteem?) and possibly even your job opportunities (impulsive? poor judgment?). Let's be real: just one stray click on a silly advertisement is unlikely to ever deny you a job. But if you click on many advertisements that trumpet pseudoscience and snake oil it may trigger something in the potential employers' algorithm that will cause it to automatically screen you out of their pool of appealing applicants—without your ever being the wiser.

Of course, your late-night Web-surfing habits are hardly the only source of data in the Reputation Economy: your interactions with your peers, colleagues, customers and vendors, dates and mates, will be collected rated, judged, scored, and stored permanently. Even data sources as seemingly disconnected as online video gaming will be integrated into your reputation profile: for example, a Minecraft or World of Warcraft strategy wizard might be cataloged as having underutilized strategic thinking skills. On the other hand, a moody player who hurls expletives and slurs after losing an online match might be tagged as being easily overheated—and run the risk of not being given preferred auto insurance rates because of an insurer's perception of increased risk of a "road rage" incident. And because storage is cheap (as we'll see in chapter 2), this data will be stored forever. So if data scientists invent some new way to analyze data (and all signs are that they will, as we'll see in chapter 3), your click today could be found to have an even more profound impact tomorrow.

The idea of being tracked *everywhere* may seem abstract, and the idea of being served up weight-loss ads after every trip to Burger King may be no worse than annoying to some people. But what happens when a life insurer starts looking at the same data to assess your life expectancy and starts rating premiums accordingly?[12] What happens when employers start looking at the data to figure out whether hiring you will affect their insurance premiums? What if the data is misinterpreted (you bought a salad) or misunderstood (maybe you bought that burger for a friend, or a homeless woman) or plain wrong (your credit card was stolen)? What happens when this data is sold to the highest bidder, for any purpose whatsoever?

And what happens when this technology is inevitably extended to facial recognition, allowing cameras in public places to track every person who enters a antiwar rally or Planned Parenthood clinic, name every person marching in the annual Pride Parade, or simply catalog every person who stumbles out of the local pub on a Saturday night? If the data can be collected, it will be, and you can bet that somebody will find a way to make money from it—if Facebook is a popular stalking tool today, imagine a site that catalogs all your interactions, whether you like it or not. There's nothing in current law stopping any of this: data publishers have enjoyed broad First Amendment protections,[13] and it's probably legal to catalog a person's public movements because there is no general "expectation of privacy" when one is out in the world. Future legal cases will have to decide at what point digital stalking gets just too creepy.

If so-called Big Data is what allows this wealth of data to be collected, it is Big Analysis that allows companies and individuals to use it in ways that affect you across all aspects of your life. The good news is that you do have the power to influence some of these decisions by carefully cultivating your own reputation, sometimes in surprising ways. Knowing how to navigate the new Reputation Economy will allow *you* to be the one to profit in a world where reputation is your most valuable asset.

So What?

The commercialization of reputation is just one part of the new Reputation Economy—a reflection of the world in which companies and governments will actively seek to profit from the measurement and sale of all forms of reputation. In the end, reputation is no different from any other commodity that can be monetized; it is inevitable that it will be commercialized, mined, refined, corrupted, bastardized, fought over, traded, sold, repackaged, stored, and used in ways never intended. Just as the quest for the oil under the sands of the Middle East has shaped the politics and history of the region, the coming fight over reputation will shape the world. If "reputation engines" run on data, control of that data will be fought over like any other valuable commodity that is unevenly distributed.

This conflict is inevitable. Computers and technology are moving faster than society can keep up; we are inventing technologies we don't yet know how to handle. The fear of technology outstripping ethics and society is not new (remember that even Albert Einstein, whose theories unlocked nuclear power, had serious reservations about atomic weaponry), but the connection to reputation is unusually personal: today's technology is making decisions that affect intimate aspects of your life— sometimes even the literally intimate aspects. Scarier still, the systems doing the scoring work under a veil of secrecy; everyday individuals have no awareness of what information is being collected, let alone how their reputation scores are calculated and used. Thus one piece of wrong information—one bad input, one false rumor, one computing error—can cause significant harm without your even knowing it. You may never even know that you are being discriminated against on the basis of your reputation; if you never receive a cold call offering the job of a lifetime, or Match.com never shows your profile to the date of your dreams, or that angel investor never offers to buy a stake in your business, you will never know that you missed out.

But the news is not all bad. Just as a poor reputation can cause you to be passed by, a *good* reputation can be your passport to myriad opportunities and benefits. Thanks to the ability of the Internet to deliver information to anyone in the world just as easily as around the corner, the break of a lifetime can come from anywhere, even thousands of miles away. Not only that, in the coming Reputation Economy a good reputation functions as a "disintermediator" of sorts—leveling the playing field by breaking down traditional gates and gatekeepers. The result is that today a complete unknown with a golden voice can parlay a popular YouTube channel into a multimillion-dollar record contract, or a faraway sports phenom can ink an athletic contract just on the basis of reputation; consider the case of Norwegian Håvard Rugland, who, having never played a single down of American football in his life, was signed to the Detroit Lions and kicked two field goals in a preseason game, thanks to the popularity of a video he posted of himself doing trick kicks with a football.

With the right reputation, the world is your oyster. Employers' algorithms will pick your résumé out of the pile of thousands just as instantaneously and robotically as they pass over the others. Banks and lenders will automatically approve you for the better rates and offers. The more appealing dates on apps and sites like Tinder, Match, and OkCupid will see your profile before they see any others. More customer prospects will come to your physical or digital store than to your competitor's. The next chapters will explore these implications of the growing Reputation Economy—and what you can do to profit from it.

Through this book you'll learn about how you can optimize

your reputation to reap all the benefits the Reputation Economy has to offer. We'll show you the secrets used to improve the lives of millions of users of Reputation.com—such as how to curate the kind of digital reputation that will make you more attractive to everyone from employers, to lenders, to insurers, to investors, and more. For example, we'll show you what keywords to put in your résumé, performance review, and LinkedIn profile to ensure that you come up at the top of recruiters' and potential employers' search results; how to curate your online and offline activity in ways that will reduce the risk profile (and therefore your premiums) calculated by insurers; how to lure venture capital for your business idea or start-up, court low interest rates from investors, and garner the attention of tech giants like Google and Microsoft. We'll even show how to create false trails and digital smoke screens to hide the negative information, or the information that doesn't match how you want to be perceived, that's out in the ether. There's nothing you can do to erase that digital footprint, but there are tricks you can use to keep it from being discovered. And we'll show how you can use all this technology to evaluate *others'* reputations so you always know whom you're dealing with, whether it's a potential employee or an investor or a romantic partner. In short, we'll show you how to become "reputation rich" in a world where your digital reputation is as valuable as the cash in your wallet.

A new digital world is coming, where the well prepared will harness the power of their digital reputations to profit and others will be left behind without knowing why. Are you prepared?

2

Stored

Reputation Is Permanent,
Cheap, and Ubiquitous

N TOMORROW'S REPUTATION ECONOMY, ALMOST EVERYTHING that is entered into the digital ether can be preserved cheaply, effortlessly, and indefinitely in one form or another. Indeed, storage of digital data has become all but free at a small scale and remarkably cheap at a large scale. Not only that, but it has become incredibly easy: now that vast amounts of data can be stored in the "cloud," you no longer need a computer science degree (or even much of a computer—an average smartphone will do) to set up databases of a size and scale that once would have taken massive physical hardware and technical expertise. The result is that massive data storage is no longer the exclusive realm of the CIA, the NSA, and other three-letter agencies, or for that matter of IBM or SAP or other three-letter companies.

Now anyone with an Amazon.com account can store a practically unlimited amount of data, and companies of all stripes—from banks to retailers to your local grocery store—are doing so. As a result, you should assume that everything you do electronically today—from surfing the Internet to conducting credit card transactions—will be recorded and stored forever.

How much more computer memory is there today? Just ask the rocket scientists: literally. Among its other feats, the spacecraft Voyager 1 is the first human-made object to leave the solar system. It was launched in 1977 with what were then six state-of-the-art mobile computers, and it left the solar system sometime in 2012 or 2013, depending on how you define the fuzzy edge of our solar neighborhood. Its six on-board computers added up to the equivalent of about 68 kilobytes of memory. By comparison, today a single top-of-the-line 2013 iPhone 5s costs hundreds of times less, fits in your pocket, and holds about 986,000 times more memory.

The start of this digital data revolution can be traced directly to the 1890 U.S. Census. At the time, the census was conducted once every ten years but took eight years to tally, meaning that the government was already gearing up to conduct the next census by the time the last one was finished. Census takers would go around to each house, write notes about the residents on a paper list, and then bring the list into massive collation centers where counters toiled to add them all up. That seemed to be the best anyone could do until Herman Hollerith, a mining engineer, presented the idea of replacing handwritten records for each household with a punched card. Prior to Hollerith, punched cards had been used to run fabric looms—never to collect data—but the government was so frustrated with the slow pace of the census, it appointed Hollerith to run the 1890 census despite his complete lack of relevant experience. The new plan worked better than even Hollerith could have imagined; the punched cards cut the time required to process the census data from eight years to one. The revelation that a person's life could be summed up on a punched card in many ways foretold the revolution in digital data that would occur a full century later, and in fact Hollerith went on to found a company that became IBM, which spent almost eighty years manufacturing punched cards and dominating the early computer market.

By the 1960s, punched cards, sometimes called Hollerith Cards, were still the state of the art for professional data storage, and had become so ubiquitous that Berkeley students wore buttons reading "Do not fold, spindle or mutilate"—a reference to the standard warning on IBM cards against damaging the cards by jabbing them onto the type of spindle sometimes used for restaurant tickets. Just across the San Francisco Bay from Berkeley, a counterculture rebel named Stewart Brand was perhaps the most ironically famous user of punched cards. In 1968, Brand published *The Whole Earth Catalog,* a literal catalog that ran more than 430 pages long and was fronted with one of the first photos of the entire Earth from space (which Brand himself lobbied NASA to release). It was intended to contain all of the supplies and information required to sustain an eco-friendly sustainable civilization, ranging from advertisements for arc welders and geodesic domes, through mathematical predictions of the flow of phosphorus through a mussel bed, through a narrative depiction of the funeral process in a Trappist community in Kentucky.

Though his catalog contained everything required to run a civilization after the collapse of computers, Brand used IBM's punched cards to manage the catalog's circulation, issuing one card per subscriber. The cards allowed him to quickly process thousands of subscriptions, print mailing labels and invoices, and create copies of his subscriber lists. In his free time, Brand was a popular techno-futurist author; he believed that mass digital data storage would widely democratize access to information and data processing. Brand's most direct impact on reputation came at a conference in 1984, at which he famously told Apple cofounder Steve Wozniak that "information wants to be free." This quote soon evolved into a key tenet of the techno-libertarian philosophy that defined the early adopters of the Internet and inspired the culture of total data collection in which we live today.

Fast-forward another fifteen years and Brand's "information wants to be free" mantra led directly to the mission statement adopted by fellow Stanford affiliates Sergey Brin and Larry Page when they founded Google: to "organize the world's information and make it universally accessible and useful." Brand's idea that information wants to be free had set the stage for instant worldwide data sharing. In other words, it was in large part due to Brand's philosophy that the very idea of unlimited access to information expanded from the types of facts and descriptions in *The Whole Earth Catalog* to eventually encompass every fact in the world, including facts about individuals.

Brand turned out to be correct, but in the meantime the problem with punched cards was that they took up an immense amount of space: a 1959 photo of a federal record-keeping warehouse shows pallets of punched cards, with forty-five boxes of cards to a pallet, adding up to around 4.3 gigabytes of total storage and taking up a warehouse at least the size of a football field.[1] Enter IBM and the "350" disk storage system, which stored data on a stack of fifty giant rotating magnetic disks. The machine was as big as a full-sized refrigerator, weighed more than one ton, and stored around 4 megabytes—just about enough to store one good photo from an average digital camera or an average-quality recording of Daft Punk's "Get Lucky." It also cost millions of dollars—or was available for lease for around $3,200 per month (in the currency of the time, or closer to $27,000 per month in today's dollars).

But just as IBM was releasing its first major disk drive product, it was also busy upgrading its biggest competition: the model 727 reel-to-reel tape system that became an icon of computing technology of the era. The 727 tape system stored data on what was basically the same tape used in cassette players (for those born after 1980, a cassette player is how people stored portable music before there were iPods or CDs).

Instead of using giant spinning disks to store data (which have the advantage of allowing very fast access), IBM's tape system stored data as magnetized spots on a long spool of magnetic tape. The benefit of a tape system is simple: storage capacity is limited only by the length of tape that can be fed into the machine. If a tape gets too long, just swap in another spool. The drawback is that it takes time—sometimes minutes or even hours—to find any particular piece of data on a long tape spool. The result is that commercial systems capable of storing data on magnetic tape are slow but truly massive in scale. As just one example, the smallest commercial model tape system made by rival manufacturer StorageTek today provides access to 1,448 cartridges of magnetic tape, storing a total of around 1.4 petabytes of data (each petabyte is 1,024 terabytes, or 1,048,576 gigabytes—or around 1,576,000,000,000,000 bytes). The largest advertised StorageTek system can store 457 petabytes of data—that's more than 1.5 gigabytes of information for every person living in the United States today. And that's just *one* storage unit; it is possible to link multiples of them together if your data storage needs are truly mind-boggling.

HOW MUCH STORAGE?

1 byte—one letter or number

1,024 bytes—1 kilobyte—half a typewritten page

1,048,576 bytes—1 megabyte—one medium-resolution photo

1,073,741,824 bytes—1 gigabyte—a full-length movie in HD

1,099,511,627,776—1 terabyte—half a research library (available in consumer devices)

1,125,899,906,842,624 bytes—1 petabyte—enough to store a high-resolution photo of every resident of the United States (available commercially)

But tape systems—and even large hard-drive farms—are big, bulky, and complex to operate. They require special electrical connections, dedicated computer servers, special fire suppression systems, raised floors for cooling and cables, a team of workers to assemble the system, and sometimes even special permitting. The tape library described above is no svelte beauty; it weighs in at a girder-crushing 15,125 pounds (6,860 kilograms), enough to require special planning to avoid turning a floor into an unplanned elevator shaft. And as it works it burns off up to 44,380 Btu per hour of waste heat—more than would be produced if you turned on an average wall-mount gas furnace and left it at full blast all day.

To demonstrate just how dramatically the world of data storage has changed since, let's compare this to one of the most ubiquitous and recognizable products out there today: the iPod Nano. The seventh-generation Nano is a rectangular music player that offers a unique mix of performance and size. About the size of a bulky wristwatch, it weighs just 31 grams (just over 1 ounce), is capable of playing twenty-four hours of music straight if fully charged, and holds 16 gigabytes of music—about the amount of data that could be contained in a bookshelf 160 yards long (about the size of a football field, including end zones), all for a retail price of $149 (in 2013 dollars). This is enough storage space to comfortably hold the address and phone number of every man, woman, and child in the United States and still have some room for workout music.

But of course, a wristwatch-sized iPod is hardly the state of the art in storage capacity. In fact, even just consumer-grade external hard drives (the kind that you can attach to a laptop or desktop computer) can store several terabytes of data—about as much as 128 iPod Nanos' worth—and are usually not much larger than a couple decks of playing cards (if the past is any guide, they will quickly shrink to fit in shirt pockets). It is estimated that a 1-terabyte disk drive could hold as much information as the paper from fifty thousand trees; 2 terabytes can store the contents of an average research library. In other words, a 5-terabyte disk drive, now available at retail to anyone with an Amazon.com account, can store about 17,500 bytes of data about every single person living in the United States—enough for a Facebook profile photo and a list of current and past addresses, with room to spare for other data. These drives cost less than $200 already, and if the trend from the last thirty years of storage technology continues, the price will keep dropping.

And this is just the amount of data the average person can store on his or her desktop computer! Today, businesses large and small can store exponentially more information in what is known as the "cloud" (the growing collection of always-online remote storage and processing facilities available through the

Internet), at virtually no cost. Thanks largely to a service provided by a little-known online retailer called Amazon.com, it is possible for any company anywhere in the world—or even any individual with a credit card or a few Bitcoin—to create a massive storage system with just a click of a mouse. There's no need for a special server room, a forklift, or assembly instructions that would make Ikea blush. All you need is a valid credit card to set up your own multiterabyte storage system in less time than it would take most people to drive to the nearest coffee shop.

It all started back in 2006, when Amazon.com CEO Jeff Bezos had a problem: Wall Street was asking for ever-higher growth, but Bezos began to realize that Amazon's business model of putting goods in boxes and shipping them around the country was beginning to show signs of reaching saturation; at some point, there must be a limit to how much stuff people would be willing to order online. At the same time, a small part of Amazon.com's development team in South Africa had become particularly good at developing technologies that allowed Amazon to use its computer servers to simultaneously handle requests from hundreds of customers per second. This allowed Amazon to use fewer computers to handle the task of serving up its website (with millions of products and around $2,750 in revenue per *second*, Amazon requires massive computing power), saving it substantial money and making it easier for Amazon to expand its computer systems as it grew.

Bezos could see that this technology had immense value—not just to Amazon's own bottom line by saving a few computer systems here and there, but potentially to other companies. The problem was that Amazon was not in the business of selling computer software; trying to sell custom installations of the software was inconsistent with the rest of Amazon's business model, which depended on reaching a mass audience. And this wasn't the kind of software you put on the "app store" for people to download; it's designed to work only on massive computer "clusters" with hundreds of interlinked machines.

But Bezos had always been a dreamer, and somehow he realized that his two problems (the need to reach a mass market for growth, and the lack of an outlet for custom software) might share a solution. Bezos (with some help) came up with the idea to essentially rent out Amazon's own raw computing power (which became known as the Elastic Computing Cloud, or EC2) and its own online storage capacity (the Simple Storage System, or S3), allowing individual customers to simply log on, create an account, and instruct Amazon's server farm to process or store any kind of data in Amazon's "cloud." In short, Amazon used its new software to reach a mass market of people who needed massive computer power but didn't want to buy and maintain their own hardware. As one commentator put it, Amazon's brilliant plan was as if Walmart were to sell access to its legendary distribution centers and logistics system and allow other retailers to use it to distribute anything from toilet paper to vaccines to car parts.

Of course, all of this storage is meaningless without something to fill it. To paraphrase the immortal words from *Field of Dreams,* "Build it and they will fill it"—and fill it they have. As of early 2013, Amazon's S3 basic online storage service stored more than 2 trillion "objects"—each roughly the equivalent of a file or database. Customers include companies ranging from Netflix—which uses Amazon's S3 storage to store and distribute more than seventeen thousand videos for its streaming service—to smaller start-ups like Heroku (more on them later), who have opted to use Amazon's services in lieu of building their own data centers, hiring their own engineering team, and generally dealing with the complexity inherent in owning heavy computer hardware.[2] The original S3 and EC2 services were a small revolution in terms of storage volume and accessibility, but they were also relatively expensive. To address the cost issue, in 2012 Amazon announced a new service called Glacier that offers all-but-free data storage with one catch: your data might not be available immediately when you request it. Amazon says that it may take up to a few hours to access any particular file, and actual users report delays of around four hours. At launch, Amazon was selling the service for around $0.01 per month per gigabyte stored—essentially offering the storage capacity of the iPod discussed above for around $0.16 per month. Some users still complain about the "high" price, but this is only $50 per month to store a 5-terabyte data collection—enough to store a small photo of every man, woman, and child living in the United States, or every tax return ever filed.

Of course, Amazon Glacier is just one of several services that allow any individual with a computer to store massive amounts of data at almost unimaginably low prices—other examples include Dropbox, which (at the time of this writing) offers all users a free 2 gigabytes of always-online storage with the option of upgrading to 100 gigabytes at the low cost of $10 per month (or $0.10 per gigabyte), and Google Drive, which allows users of Gmail Picasa and other Google services to store a free 15 gigabytes' worth of e-mails, photos, and more. Even Flickr, the popular photo-sharing service (owned by Yahoo!), now offers every free account holder 1 *terabyte* of storage, or enough for about six hundred thousand average-sized photos. And these data stores are growing all the time—Google historically placed a counter on the Gmail home page showing that its free storage was constantly increasing, and the move to 15 gigabytes was a threefold increase over its previous limit of "merely" 5 gigabytes in 2012.

The sum total of all this storage is immense: one study estimated that total worldwide digital data stores had exceeded 295 *billion* gigabytes as early as 2007.[3] As one researcher put it, "If we were to take all that information and store it in books, we could cover the entire area of the US or China in 13 layers of books."[4]

In short, today, for a fraction of the cost of an iPod, companies can store massive troves of data about you, ranging from a history of the advertisements you've clicked on (including what site you were visiting, what time of day it was, and whether you ultimately made a purchase from the advertiser), to a history of transactions with your toll transponder (revealing virtually everywhere you've traveled by car), to credit card purchases, to every photo of you uploaded to Facebook (whether you uploaded the photo or a friend did), and more.

Free Like Dirt

The real implication of the plummeting price of data storage—and the shocking one at that—is that it is now cheaper and easier to keep most data than to delete it. Deleting data takes tough business decisions: *What if we need that data later? What if there's value in it? What if we accidentally delete an active customer's orders?* And even once the decision to delete is made, it takes a computer programmer and sometimes a database engineer to actually do it. In an ideal world, every database is carefully designed to allow easy deletion of old data. But in reality most databases are pieced together over time with little consideration of how to delete data later; if a database is complex, it will take tens of hours (or more) for a programmer to untangle the old data from the new and tease out just the parts that are no longer wanted.

Hiring a programmer skilled enough to work with such a complex database can easily cost more than $100 per hour, and rates only go up from there. Assuming a very small database—maybe a small website with a few thousand customers—it might take ten hours (an extremely favorable estimate, which assumes that the database is overall well designed) to tease apart the database to identify how to delete a bunch of old records. That's at least $1,000 in just programming time, not to mention lost opportunities and distraction; it can easily run much higher if there aren't backup tapes (slow) or other "offline" copies of the data, which can add hours (if not more) to a project. For a database like Facebook's, which is stored over many different server farms with trillions of records, making even small changes outside the database design can cost hundreds of thousands of dollars (if not more).

It wasn't that long ago that this $1,000 it cost to delete data from a simple database would buy only 800,000 bytes of new storage, or less than a Facebook profile photo (a $500 disk drive was the standard for Apple Macintosh computers through the 1980s, and it held a laughably small amount by today's standards). Given the high cost of storage (relative to today), this was a time when deleting data made sense as a strategy to preserve space. But today, for a company maintaining its own storage solutions, $1,000 will buy (at press time) more than 20 terabytes of hard-drive space permanently—more than 40 million times more storage than the Macintosh drive. If a company is willing to use tape storage, $1,000 will buy five times that, or around 100 terabytes of tape storage.[5] And prices for storage are falling so fast that if you buy a computer today with a 1-terabyte drive, when the time comes to replace the computer, much larger drives will be available for the same price. So why would a company ever bother deleting data if it's infinitely cheaper to just buy more storage?

The result has been that the default has become to save digital data indefinitely rather than delete it. And this doesn't just apply to the information you post on Facebook or store on your personal computer. Your work e-mail is likely to be preserved in backup tapes for years unless your employer has a reason to delete it (though smart employers do develop e-mail destruction policies as a prudent counterbalance to the tendency for digital data to hang around forever). Your work projects, whether presentations, reports, financial projections, or PowerPoints (not to mention any personal information you unwisely save on your work computer), are likely stored on some company drive somewhere for perpetuity—once again, if the hard drive fills up, buying a replacement drive will be far cheaper and easier than picking through thousands of old files to figure out which can be deleted and which need to be saved. A search of a major law firm's file storage system reveals hundreds of documents from the 1980s still available with just a click, even well into the 2010s—why would any lawyer at the firm (who bills at hundreds of dollars per hour) invest hundreds of hours of her valuable time trying to identify which documents are still relevant and which are not?

Your personal e-mail, too, is now being stored indefinitely. Before Google introduced Gmail in 2004, many webmail providers would allow only 10 megabytes of storage. Microsoft's popular Hotmail service allowed only 2 megabytes of storage, less than one modern digital photo.[6] Under these small limits, users had to constantly delete e-mails in order to have storage space available for incoming mail. In a way, people got used to treating e-mail like postal mail: reading their incoming messages and then immediately trashing most of them, perhaps saving only the most important messages. Mail providers (like Hotmail) even included a prominent "delete message" button to assist users in the Sisyphean task of e-mail inbox cleansing.

That all changed in 2004 when Gmail launched, announcing that its users would receive 1 gigabyte of storage—over one hundred times the prevailing standard and five hundred times what Microsoft offered. Tellingly, Google replaced the "delete" button with an "archive" button, a way to move old e-mails out of the inbox without deleting them and instead to store them permanently in the Gmail cloud (just in case you ever need that "funny" e-mail your aunt forwarded in 2006—the one from her AOL account, with the terrible puns—be assured, it has been archived). And over the years, Google has steadily increased the amount of e-mail storage available to users; for years, it slightly increased the total storage *each day,* and now it offers a combined storage limit of *15 gigabytes* along with its other "cloud" products. Other e-mail providers have followed suit, expanding their storage limits and making the "archive" button more prominent than "delete." By making it more difficult to delete e-mail than to keep it (it's still possible, but the "delete" button is hard to find), Google changed users' expectations about how digital data will be treated and cemented user expectations that data will be around forever.

Facebook has similarly expanded its storage capacity over the years, finding it much easier and more cost effective to simply buy new storage than to delete data. Facebook buys new hard drives at a pace fast enough to store every profile that is added, every photo that is posted, every message that is sent, and every ad that is clicked by its 1+ billion global users, adding an additional 500 terabytes of storage every day. That means that *every* day, Facebook adds to its databases fifty times the amount of data in the Library of Congress's print collections. Even the information you take down from your public page is still likely being stored *somewhere:* when requested by law enforcement, Facebook can create a digital dossier that for some users runs more than eighty pages and includes not only the information you might expect (photos, status messages, and the like) but data that is not publicly visible, like people whom you have "unfriended," wall posts that you think have been deleted, recent IP (network) addresses used to log in, a list of pages viewed, and so forth. Some data experts believe that Facebook doesn't actually delete a photo from its servers, even if the owner clicks the "Delete Photo" button.[7] And Twitter? Not only does Twitter generate over 400 million tweets of data every day, the U.S. Library of Congress is even permanently storing every public tweet sent on Twitter, regardless of its contents.

The same goes for data from countless other domains. We've reached a point where the safest assumption is that every digital interaction you have is being *permanently* recorded in at least one place. It might not all be analyzed yet (soon, see chapter 3) or put to use (chapters 4 and 7), but it's out there somewhere, archived permanently, waiting to surface when you least expect it. This goes for all your financial transactions, from credit score inquiries to ATM withdrawals to stock trades. It goes for every word that's ever been written about your company or business ranging from blog posts to tweets to formal press releases. It goes for all your government records—every property tax payment is public and archived in some states, and in others every mug shot from every arrest is put online and archived across dozens of sites, regardless of guilt, innocence, or completely wrongful arrest. It goes for every review you've ever posted online about every hotel, movie, book, or restaurant and every Instagram photo taken tableside; plus plenty of juicy metadata—like your location—that you might not realize your smartphone is embedding in the images. For years, major online advertisers kept a detailed record of your every click, indefinitely; only regulatory pressure caused them to start to remove your name from (but not delete) the data after a few months.

Every credit card purchase you've made—on- or offline—is tracked and permanently stored not only by your credit card company but by the seller's payment processor (and then is often sold to other retailers). Every pharmaceutical prescription filled is entered into a giant prescribing database that itself was the subject of a Supreme Court lawsuit. Your online dating profile from your twenties (with those embarrassing ironic references) remains on some server somewhere, long after you've happily married and produced three beautiful children. Every cell phone tower to which your phone connects creates a permanent digital trail immortalizing, quite literally, your every step. All the websites you view each day from your phone and home Internet connections, security camera footage from many public places—the list goes on.

Even data directly related to your career growth is tracked and stored, forever. Even if you aren't on LinkedIn, your friends and colleagues who are have inevitably allowed it to access their address books and automatically listed you as a coworker, which gives a sophisticated computer algorithm a big clue as to your progress through an organization. Your salary history is stored by your employer's payroll processor; it's not known how it is used yet, but it's all kept. There's a record kept of every posting you've made about your job—even if you think you've done it anonymously, it can still be traced back, especially now that increasingly powerful software can often identify you by nothing more than the quirks of your writing style.

Ever drive down a rural road and see signs for "Free Dirt"?

They exist because dirt is everywhere and nearly impossible to dispose of—it's easy to find, easy to keep, and hard to remove. Most people end up just leaving it around if they excavate it; and big heaps of dirt can last centuries. In some areas of the United States, there are still heaps of dirt that were used as fortifications during the Civil War; in Illinois, there are even dirt mounds left by the Cahokia native group before 1400 A.D. Dirt seems to stick around forever. Your data, like dirt, is here to stay: it's easy to accumulate and hard to get rid of.

The most obvious result of this revolution in digital storage is that blemishes on your reputation will live on indefinitely. Even a one-time mistake will follow you forever if it takes place in the digital realm—and what doesn't these days? Did a video of you snapping at a customer during your worst day end up on YouTube? Did you get caught reviewing your own business? Or did a nosy neighbor with Google Glass catch you enjoying a candlelit dinner with a stranger while your husband was on a business trip—and post a picture of it to Facebook? Worse, that data has so much staying power that our digital reputations are often tarnished by mistakes we didn't even make!

Take, for example, the 2012 "McDonald's spitting incident," in which an employee at a South Carolina outpost of the fast-food chain was charged with food tampering for allegedly spitting in customers' drinks. Though criminal charges were dropped because the allegations were never proved (and in fact are now suspected to be fake), a Google search for the employee's name years later still brings up articles related to the incident. His reputation will be forever marred by literally dirty allegations.

In California, equally troubling, there have been reports that parents who were tentatively placed on the state's list of child abusers have not been removed from the list even after being exonerated—one couple in Valencia, California, took a case to the Supreme Court of the United States and were still unable to remove their names even though the lower courts agreed that they were "factually innocent."[8]

What's more, these days information starts going on your digital permanent record at an alarmingly early age. In the United Kingdom, the government has actually created a database of schoolchildren who call each other derogatory names. The goal is to allow coordination of records when students move between districts, but the government has kept mum on the deletion policy for the database, so it is entirely possible that these records will follow these children into their adult lives. Again, like dirt, this data is easier to gather than to get rid of.

Similarly, even actions taken by others *against* you will be permanent. Take as an example bullying: being perceived as a victim of bullying can unfairly prejudice others against you or focus their perception on your victimhood. For example, a Google search for "Karen Klein" today includes results such as "Bullied Bus Monitor Karen Klein" and "Karen Klein, Bullied Bus Monitor." These results spring from a 2012 incident in which Ms. Klein, then sixty-eight years old and partially deaf, was working part time as a school bus monitor. A group of seventh-grade students began mercilessly taunting Ms. Klein—prodding her, calling her fat, and going as far as to (perhaps unknowingly) mock her for the suicide of her eldest son—while another videotaped the incident for later upload to YouTube. For the foreseeable future, anybody who searches for her name will read about how she was a victim of bullying—rather than about her years of service in the community or anything about the other sixty-seven years of her life.

And the permanence of our digital reputations has a much bigger impact than just what appears in Google results. Even incidents that would never appear on Google, like sending an intemperate e-mail to a colleague, missing a credit card payment, taking more debt than you can handle, making late-night infomercial purchases, or getting busted for "borrowing" your neighbor's wireless or cable, can be easily accessed by reputation engines, triggering a black mark on your permanent digital record.

This goes even beyond one-time incidents like a late payment or a wrongful complaint. Long-term patterns of behavior, even ones that may seem completely normal or harmless to you now—are being recorded and stored forever. For example, the city of San Francisco is equipping all 819 of its municipal buses with digital cameras to snap photos of cars blocking bus lanes,[9] and a firm called Vigilant Solutions collects data from hundreds of video cameras used by repo agents to search for target vehicles, merges the data into a giant shared database, and allows law enforcement to access it. As of 2010, the database contained more than 185 million vehicle location records, and 23 million new records were being added each month. For better or worse, for alibi or for guilt, a private company may have a very detailed record of your whereabouts over time.[10]

Anywhere, Anytime

In the world of permanent digital data storage, you should also assume that anything stored about you can crop up in any new context at any time. This is because, in the Reputation Economy, the boundaries between your various "worlds" are quickly diminishing. It may seem that using an online dating site is reasonably anonymous: usually only a first name or a nickname is displayed, and most dating sites give advice for keeping your identity safe and private. But one blogger has already identified a technique that leverages public facial recognition tools to find users of Match.com on Facebook, just on the basis of their photos—even if the Match users don't provide full names.[11] Once Facebook caught wind of the technique, they didn't sue or block it—they actually *bought* the facial recognition vendor in question and shut the service down. For now, the software is offline, but imagine what uses Facebook might have for photo recognition in the future.

Dating sites aren't the only ones with alarmingly permeable databases. A company named Ark recently raised $4.2 million in a seed fund-raising round to aggregate and merge data from social networks like Facebook and LinkedIn and connect it to news and Web information. A company called Spokeo has been collecting and connecting public records with social networking profiles for years—pay a few dollars and the Spokeo service will often provide both a home address and a link to the person's Facebook or LinkedIn profile. If your online banking service uses a prior address or a zip code as a security question, Spokeo has rendered it insecure. No matter where your information lives on the Internet, once it's out there, not only is it permanent, but it can crop up anywhere, when you least expect it.

At the end of the day, many people say, "So what?" Everyone has a past. Everyone has done something embarrassing. Some people honestly believe that one day we'll all get over it: we'll realize that everyone has a history, and our digital permanent records will become nothing more than blips on our digital pasts with no consequences or bearing on our present, offline lives. But recent years have shown that if that day comes it'll be a long time from now. For as long as companies can legally use all this data to hire the best candidates, identify the worst credit risks, charge higher fees and premiums to vulnerable customers, and more—they will. Rather than fighting it, your best option is to curate the kind of digital permanent record that will put you on the right side of this reputation divide.

Thankfully, even in the world of permanent digital storage, there are some things we can do to protect ourselves from the omnipresent agents of Big Data and Big Analysis. The first is obvious: always assume that *everything* you do electronically is being recorded and stored forever. And, if you want to be safe, assume that ever-present recording extends to any activity outside your home, whether online or not.

Second, be very careful about any confessions of wrongdoing you might be tempted to make. We get that unburdening your sins on Facebook may feel liberating, but in the Reputation Economy, where even the most minor admissions made today may hang around forever, you may want to think twice before tweeting about how you charged your tropical vacation to your corporate AmEx, or how you cheated on your graduate entrance exam. To take a more serious example, let's say you are falsely accused of a minor ethical foible at work, like taking home office supplies against company policy or showing up late a few days in a row, and your boss offers not to take any action if you simply admit your mistake. In the predigital era, owning up (even if you didn't do it) might have been the path of least resistance. But in the digital age, you should assume that records of your (false) confession will be kept forever and will surface when you apply for another job. Think that sounds extreme? It's already happening: a company called First Advantage Corporation sells a database—with the Orwellian name Esteem—that consists of a list of retail employees who have admitted to stealing product even if no criminal charges were ever filed.[12] When considering an applicant, major retailers like Target, CVS, and Family Dollar include the Esteem database as part of their background check. As the *New York Times* reports, "Many [employees] have no idea that they admitted committing a theft or that the information will remain in databases"—and why should they when they are offered a simple deal with their boss to make everything go away?

Being "on the record" for admitting to a misdeed you didn't commit can have even graver consequences. In recent years there has been political outrage when people charged years ago with minor crimes who pleaded nolo contendere—legal Latin for roughly "I'm not going to bother to fight this"—have later been denied green cards or gun permits. In the years before the Reputation Economy, a conviction written up only in local hard-copy files could have entirely escaped notice for decades, but ever since state convictions started being stored in digital databases, these records have become impossible to escape.

Finally, there are ways of creating digital smoke screens to push the information you don't want discovered way down in your search results. The first step is to identify the type of information that is creating a problem. If it's public search results (things that appear in Google, Bing, Yahoo!, and the like), then you're in luck: it's possible to drown them out by posting as much positive "noise"—professional rewards won, health and fitness goals attained, and so on—as you can.

Either way, create as many smoke screens as you can. To counter false, misleading, outdated, or unduly overemphasized information that appears in public Web results, the basic playbook has been published by Reputation.com and others: create *lots* of positive content (we mean *lots*) about yourself, publish it widely, and repeat until search engines and reputation engines are so overwhelmed by the positive that they disregard the negative as a fluke or aberration. Create public profiles on sites like Twitter, LinkedIn, Facebook, Tumblr, and Pinterest, as well as any sites relevant to interests that you are willing to make part of your public profile (such as *Daily Kos* or *Huffington Post* if you are into liberal politics and comfortable making your views public, or industry-specific sites for your career). Make sure these profiles have enough information that an automated computer could connect them together (list the same geographic area in each, and tie some background points such as a school or an employer in each—even if they aren't actually true, be consistent), and then just keep publishing. Set up a persona you are comfortable with publicly, one that you will not be offended by if computers or humans read it.

And don't rule out the absurd; computers are still "dumb" in many ways. For example, suppose you have been falsely flagged as having a concern about fitness or health. You could buy Fitbit, a glorified pedometer that tracks how much you move and then uploads the data to a public online profile that shows how much you exercise. Then if you want to be really sneaky, snap that Fitbit to your dog (or, if your dog is as lazy as one of the authors', your kids, or a paint shaker), and you'll quickly be the fittest person in your town (at least according to the Internet). Be sure to make your Fitbit profile public, link it to your Facebook profile, use the same profile picture on the Fitbit site and on your professional network (such as LinkedIn), and otherwise help the reputation algorithms get the hint. Unfair? Probably, but it may be the only way to undo an unfair mistake made against you. Or you could start posting photos of your coworkers' salads on Instagram while you chow down on french fries. Maybe the reputation engines will eventually get wise to these tricks, but not today.

If you're a business or a professional of any kind (from a hairdresser to a high-end strategist), collect reviews from your most enthusiastic customers. Many sites look for a combination of volume of reviews (the more reviews you have, the higher you rank) and quality of reviews (the more stars, on average, you get, the higher you rank). Find customers who are enthusiastic—whether by asking them how their experience was, or by your own survey, or just by looking at what they purchased—and encourage them to leave reviews. Of course, the U.S. Federal Trade Commission requires disclosure if you pay people to leave a review, but there is no prohibition on giving a coupon and then separately asking for a review; we actually don't encourage exchange of value for reviews, but many businesses do this, as they have done in survey processes for decades. Sites like Yelp and Google Plus are obvious choices, but consider industry-specific sites too (like Angie's List for home repairs and other home owner services). Consider too the employment side of the business—sites like Glassdoor rank businesses on the basis of employee rankings, and your recruiting may be severely affected by a negative Glassdoor ranking.

Preserve your privacy and stop the flow of potentially damaging information (everything can be damaging when taken out of context, and attitudes that are common today may be taboo in twenty years) to the best of your ability. Keep your personal thoughts personal by making sure your personal Twitter and Facebook feeds are hard to find—lock your personal thoughts down from public view and create separate public personas that are not objectionable. One recent privacy trend on Facebook is for individuals to rename their "personal" profiles to a variant on their name that friends will recognize and computers will not ("Michael Frtk" or "Mchl Firtek" or the like), then locking the entire profile to friends-only. It's not perfect—eventually, computers will figure this trick out too—but it's a layer of protection that's better than nothing. At the same time, some people are creating new public profiles with nonobjectionable work-related content, under their full name and published with full visibility to the world, to create a false trail. While these practices technically violate Facebook's terms of service, Facebook has shown no interest in stopping it: Facebook gets to claim an increased number of active users for every person who creates "personal" and "public" profiles. One important note: if you do begin to divide up the world between "personal" and "public," be careful to restrict all of your photos to one side or the other—any photo of you that appears in your "public" profile should not appear in your "personal" profile, and vice versa.

There has recently been an explosion of software and apps that are designed to delete messages after they are viewed or after a certain time, like the popular messaging service Snapchat (frequently but not exclusively used by teens to send each other gossip, rumors, love notes, and nude pictures that are automatically deleted after the recipient sees them). These are far from perfect—in early 2014 a hacker figured out a way to download the phone numbers connected to Snapchat user names—but they're better than nothing. Just don't become overconfident that your messages are secure; even if Snapchat makes it difficult to save messages, nothing stops your recipient (or an intruder) from taking a picture of whatever you send. For more serious use, there are secure messaging services like TigerText that can be set to permanently and irrevocably delete messages after receipt—perfect for fleeting chats inside a business or organization. If you want even more security, the Telegram app claims to use military-grade encryption that even the organization's founders can't break. As of this writing, they've pledged a $200,000 reward if someone can break the app's encryption.

The point is that protecting your reputation requires a vigilance far beyond paying cash for embarrassing purchases rather than using a credit card, deleting inappropriate Facebook photos, and making intemperate comments online under an alias rather than your own name. All these activities can be digitally traced today with enough effort—and that amount of effort is ever decreasing.

So while black marks on your digital record can never be deleted, there are ways to keep them from being readily uncovered. Throughout the rest of the book we'll let you in on more sneaky ways to drown out the negatives with the positives, hide the information you don't want discovered, and paint your permanent digital persona in the best possible light.

3

Scored

Everything That Can Be Collected
and Aggregated Will

S O WE KNOW THAT EVERY DAY A MASSIVE TROVE OF IN-
formation about you is being collected and stored—
permanently. But in and of itself the collection of data is not
terribly meaningful—what really matters is what people do with
it. Even in a world where every detail of your waking life is captured (perhaps a tiny "drone" aircraft follows you around with a
high-resolution camera), if all of that data gets locked away in a
massive dusty warehouse buried under layers of bureaucracy—
a box where items go to disappear—there is only so much damage it can do. In that world, both the risk and the value associated
with your personal information are pretty limited: it might get
pulled out if, say, you get arrested or audited, but otherwise it'll
quietly languish in obscurity, and no one will be the wiser.

The good news is that today's methods of data collection aren't yet quite as obtrusive as a tiny drone (though they're getting close). The bad news is that the data that *is* collected about you isn't being stowed away in some obscure and secure box somewhere either. To the contrary; it is being put to use every day. Because not only is the *storage* of data becoming cheap, ubiquitous, and permanent, as we read in the preceding chapter, but new and emerging technologies are also making it simpler, easier, and cheaper to *analyze and quantify and draw conclusions from* this data than ever before.

As we've seen in previous chapters, in today's Reputation Economy there exist huge troves of data to be mined for information about everything from our purchasing habits to our work performance to our financial history and much more. But making *predictions* about our future behavior—like what product we're likely to buy next or how productive an employee we'll be or our likelihood of paying back a loan—involves aggregating, filtering, and analyzing that data with a level of precision and sophistication that has only recently become possible. Sorting through and parsing these massive data sets to find useful and predictive information used to take massive computing power applied in a brute-force and not entirely methodical way; until recently there was no good system that allowed computers to answer complex questions or make reliable predictions based on these data sets. But that is all changing, and it's changing fast.

In 2004, two engineers at Google—Jeffrey Dean and Sanjay Ghemawat—released a paper describing, in engineer-speak, "a simple and powerful interface that enables automatic parallelization and distribution of large-scale computations, combined with an implementation of this interface that achieves high performance on large clusters of commodity PCs."[1] In plain English, they had figured out a way to use hundreds or even thousands of small computers (rather than one impossibly large computer) to answer difficult questions using huge sets of raw data (and had published the leading paper on it).

Think of the old model of data analysis—one large computer trying to solve an entire problem by itself—as being like one person taking a one-hundred-question multiple-choice exam. The new model proposed by Dean and Ghemawat, in contrast, would be equivalent to dividing that long exam among one hundred students, with each student answering one question and then compiling them with all the others to assemble one answer sheet. In other words, with Dean and Ghemawat's system, just as an exam that would take hours for one person to finish could be completed in minutes by a team; a data set that would take a single computer hours to analyze could now be parsed in minutes, or even seconds, by a fleet of machines. They called the process of dividing up and answering the questions Map and the process of putting the answers back together Reduce and configured their system so that any computer could perform either the Map function (dividing up questions to be answered and working on them) or the Reduce function (putting the answers back together).

This wasn't the first time somebody had thought of using multiple computers in parallel to solve a problem, but it was one of the most elegant and easy to use. In fact, it was so much easier that it opened the field up to a new world of casual engineers. Furthermore, their system was powerful enough to Map and Reduce data sets far, far larger than the equivalent of a one-hundred-question multiple-choice test—think of teams of thousands of students automatically dividing into smaller teams and subteams to solve massively long and complex open-ended test questions. Some students would automatically start assigning problems to their peers, others would work on answering them, and others would collect the results. Best of all, their roles could switch at any time—assigners could become answerers and vice versa, depending on what was needed more at the time.

As an example of what MapReduce could do, when a group of computer scientists at Google wanted to create a simple visual shape recognition system (a very basic form of computer vision) without all of the work of actually coding a computer to recognize shapes, they instead created a computer algorithm that just saw images as a mass of pixels, with no hints as to what to look for in an image. They then used a system similar to MapReduce to create a cluster of one thousand computers. Over three days, the engineers fed the cluster 10 million images from the Internet and asked the computer system to look for patterns. The computers came up with a variety of them, the most impressive of which included a recognition system that could distinguish cats from human bodies or faces—with accuracy better than many systems that had been painstakingly created with detailed rules.[2] (It tells you something about what people are posting online if the first thing a completely unguided computer learned to distinguish was pictures of people from pictures of cats.)

It wasn't long before an engineer named Doug Cutting found a way to put this technology to practical and public use. Cutting was attempting to build a free and "open-source" search engine that would be a competitor to Google, only instead of using Google's "closed-source" software (Google closely guards the code that runs its search engine), he would make both his source code and his actual working search engine available to anyone who wanted it. He called the system Nutch. Shortly after the MapReduce paper was released, Cutting and his colleague Mike Cafarella realized that the MapReduce innovation could dramatically improve the speed of the Nutch engine by enabling many small computers to undertake the massive project of indexing all the pages on the Internet—a task that had previously required the use of one massive and prohibitively expensive computer.

It took a massive rewrite of the Nutch code base to incorporate the idea of MapReduce, but once they did it the Nutch team noticed an immediate improvement in Nutch's speed; with MapReduce, the Nutch system could read and analyze hundreds of millions of pages per month. And the system seemed as though it could scale indefinitely: the only thing holding the team back from analyzing billions of pages was funding to buy more computers or a faster Internet connection.[3]

Clearly, Nutch never really took off as a competitor to Google (how many times have you heard someone say, "I Nutched you"?), but some of the innovations spurred by Nutch have gone on to make as big of an impact on the world of data analysis as Google has to the world of search. Nutch still exists as an open-source software project, but its real impact on the world of digital has been through its spin-off project: a software system called Hadoop. (In case you are wondering, the "Hadoop" name came from the name of Cutting's son's stuffed elephant—he says he chose the name because it was "short, relatively easy to spell and pronounce, meaningless, and not used elsewhere.")[4]

Essentially, Hadoop brought terabyte-scale data analysis to the masses—or at least a lot closer to the masses. Before Hadoop, any true mass-scale data analysis project required writing a heap of computer code even beyond the MapReduce concept, such as monitoring the progress of hundreds or thousands of individual computers and reassembling the individual results into a coherent whole. With Hadoop, all of the "overhead" is automated—Hadoop takes care of distributing the work, assembling the results, keeping redundant copies of data, and verifying that every task is on track to be completed. The Hadoop software package even handles lots of little complexities that you might not even realize exist—for example, it matches worker computers with data that is stored as physically close as possible, increasing the system's speed and minimizing network congestion. What's more, because Cutting published the Hadoop system to the world as free and open-source software, any company with the computing power could now analyze virtually limitless sets of data with minimal overhead costs or effort.

Thanks to these innovations, the Hadoop system proved more powerful and popular than perhaps even Cutting anticipated. In 2007, not long after its release, Facebook began using it to organize and extract meaning from its massive set of user data.[5] By 2008, Facebook had installed a Hadoop system that used more than 2,500 computers working in parallel to analyze data like site statistics and usage.[6] And by 2012, Facebook announced it was using a Hadoop system to parse a database that had grown to more than 100 petabytes and was growing by roughly half a petabyte per day[7] (remember, 100 petabytes is around 2 billion filing cabinets' worth of data—long enough to stretch to the moon and back three times, or, put another way, enough to store around 1,300 years of HDTV)—all using a largely off-the-shelf system that is freely available for anyone to download and use.

Hundreds of other companies have since embraced Hadoop, from Amazon.com, which uses it to find patterns in millions of purchases in order to make product recommendations; to LinkedIn, which uses it to suggest "People You May Know"; to Yahoo!, which runs Hadoop on a total of forty thousand computer systems to filter spam, personalize your home page, and analyze advertising trends, among other tasks.[8] eBay uses a five-hundred-computer Hadoop cluster to analyze popular sellers and items, as well as for other undisclosed purposes.[9] Zions Bancorporation uses a Hadoop cluster to analyze transactions for potential fraud, and start-up ipTrust uses a Hadoop system to assign a "trust score" to every IP address (network address) on the Internet, again for fraud detection.[10] Even the U.S. military has gotten in on the trend: through contractor Digital Reasoning, the armed forces use an unspecified number of computers to analyze correlations across intelligence documents.[11]

Other data analysis companies, like Texas-based Delphi Analytics, have not publicly stated that they use Hadoop, but they do use similar methods to analyze massive data sets about consumers. Delphi helps lenders model what they call the "performance" of loans—basically, to predict whether they'll get paid back or not. The company builds custom "behavioral scoring algorithms" that match hundreds of variables for each loan with similar loans that have and have not been paid back—and then uses this data to try to predict which customers will and won't default. They use everything from "the relative wealth of a customer within their lot-and-block" to the fuel economy of a customer's car to build models, but they have recently branched into social networking data as well. In their words, "With social network information, there is a wealth of . . . information available . . . which groups they affiliate with, which special interests they indicate, which industries their 'connections' claim, their level of engagement with the social media itself," and so on.[12] Do other people who are on Facebook 24/7 fail to pay back their loans? We can't confirm or deny, but it's a safe bet you'll get a closer eye from a Delphi-enabled lender if you're also an avid social network user. If you "Like" a Facebook group that's filled with bad credit risks, you'll also get special attention. In other words, Delphi takes data gleaned from your social network, uses a "behavioral scoring algorithm" to compare you to thousands of other borrowers, and scores you on your likelihood of paying back your loans. And they are far from alone—the same methods are being applied across tens of industries.

In short, with the cost of analyzing massive troves of data heading toward zero, companies and individuals alike can mine our digital traces with greater speed, precision, and depth than ever. The result? Welcome to a world of reputation scores.

Everything Will Be Scored

Computers are terribly literal machines. A computer can add up an almost infinite string of numbers in milliseconds, but it will never understand the beauty of a sunset, the emotion of childbirth, or the pride of victory. This makes sense given that, at least for the foreseeable future, computers work entirely with numbers; after all, at its essence, computer code is nothing more than strings of binary digits.

With that in mind, it should come as no surprise that a computer thinks of you as just a series of numbers: every photo you post, every website you visit, every piece of information you provide to a computer with a click of your mouse is reduced to a number that its algorithms can manipulate. The machine means no insult, but it has no other way to represent you—its understanding is limited to math.

So it stands to reason that computers would rely on numerical scoring to organize and make sense of all the data they are fed. After all, a computer can't form judgments the way humans do, but it *can* calculate whether a certain number (a trust score, for example) is higher or lower than another number. A computer can't make a moral judgment about whether you are a good or bad person, but it can, for example, add up the number of your reported charitable donations, subtract the number of your reported arrests or penalties for tax evasion, count the number of references to cheating and lying on your Facebook page, and assign you a numerical "morality" score as a result.

Given how cheaply and easily computers can now parse all the data that makes up our digital footprint—thanks to software like Hadoop and others—it is inevitable that soon we will all have numerical scores assigned to us for every trait that anybody wants to measure. If a retailer wants to know how likely you are to buy a new designer handbag, for example, they might ask the computer to calculate your disposable income score (based on your financial status and past spending history) along with maybe a customer loyalty score and a fashionista score—each based on your online activity and your susceptibility to different forms of advertising. Similarly, if a life insurance company wants to know what premium to offer you, it could easily assign you a health score based on the frequency of your doctor visits, the duration of your gym membership, the number of monthly credit card charges to the Cheesecake Factory, and any other factors its algorithms know to be connected to health and longevity. In short, any company—or even any individual—can assign you a "reputation score" (similar to a credit score) on any of thousands of dimensions ranging from your credibility to your social awareness to your political engagement to your compatibility as a friend or a romantic partner.

Reputation scoring may be scary, but it isn't inherently bad. In fact, it can be a useful way to make sense of huge data sets that might have thousands or millions of different events, or more. Just as a football game is represented as a final score instead of hundreds of different plays or tens of thousands of different decisions by players, a reputation score can be a neat and easy way to summarize thousands of individual preferences and decisions. Instead of listing every advertisement you have ever clicked on and every advertisement you have ignored (probably hundreds of thousands of them by now), a score can simply give a snapshot of how frequently and on what kind of advertisements you click. It's easy to see the appeal of this kind of numerical scoring—it's fast, it's unambiguous, and it allows *people* to believe that they are making decisions based on quantitative factors without all of the messiness that comes with human biases in judgment. The problem is that just as the final score of a football game can be misleading (for example, a game that appears to be a blowout on paper only because the winning team scored two fluke touchdowns in the last five minutes), reputation scores can be equally misleading—perhaps somebody borrowed your laptop, or you were clicking on ads for market research rather than to purchase, or any of a thousand other factors that computers can't understand or process.

So how pervasive, exactly, will this type of reputation scoring become, and why does it matter? Well, consider that *job scores* will inevitably be one of the first widely publicized scores. We'll discuss job scores more in chapter 4, but the general principle is that employers and potential employers' computers will soon be parsing hundreds or even thousands of data points to issue scores predicting how loyal and productive an employee you'll be. If these score are low, you may be offered a far lower starting salary, or you may not even be offered the job at all. By the same token, being perceived as *overly* loyal may be disadvantageous: if your employer thinks you are in the top 10 percent of productive employees but also staggeringly loyal, he may be tempted to underpay you or deny you a promotion in favor of somebody else who is less loyal and more likely to leave unless he or she gets promoted. The scariest part about all of it is that since all this scoring is happening behind closed doors you could be getting bypassed for potential raises or opportunities or promotions on the basis of a poor score without even knowing it.

Companies already issue *customer value* scores—a measure of whether you're likely to spend money on anything from luxury goods to discount retail, and from payday loans to traditional banking products. A company in St. Cloud, Minnesota, called eBureau calls its product eScores and claims to be able to rate potential customers for online retailers—usually in less than a second.[13] How extensive is eBureau's data? The company claims to access "billions of records across thousands of databases that cover nearly all US adults and households," and it "adds over 3 billion new records each month," including your "Internet, catalog and direct marketing purchase histories."[14] Ever call a 1-800 number for customer service and feel like you're at the back of the longest line at Disney World ("your estimated wait time: two hours and fifty-five minutes")? Thank companies like eBureau that allow retailers to predict if you are likely a hot prospect (instant answers to your calls) or a broke complainer (welcome to the queue, good luck staying on the line until somebody feels like answering) before they even pick up.

Similarly, companies will soon be issuing *credibility scores,* which they'll use to determine your eligibility to participate in social sharing services like car sharing, apartment sharing, and so on. Imagine a service that allowed you to land at an airport and pick up a stranger's car, at half the price of a traditional rental (and without the rental car smell). With a high credibility score—based on squeaky-clean credit, an accident-free driving record, and a history of always paying all your bills in full—your risk to a potential car lender is relatively low. With a low credibility score, however, the company or individual running the sharing service may very well charge you a higher price or decide not to rent to you at all.

Then there are *health and longevity scores,* issued by everyone from insurers to investors to employers. One firm, Rigi Capital Partners, is already using a macabre scoring system to identify potential customers who are likely to die sooner (and thus be eligible for life insurance payout sooner). It then buys life insurance policies from those customers. The customer gets a cash payment while still alive, and Rigi Capital Partners gets the life insurance payment when the customer dies. To make this rather morbid prediction about which customers will be quickest to croak, the company's algorithms review not only the typical medical data but Facebook photos and posts for signs of the customer's vitality—or lack thereof. If the customer's Facebook page suggests that he or she is socially active and vibrant—attending rock concerts, going on skiing trips, that sort of thing—Rigi is substantially less likely to invest, on the belief that socially active applicants are more likely to live longer (and thus that Rigi will not be paid quickly for their policies).[15]

Companies also exist that try to identify sick individuals on the basis of their habits and then sell this information to health care companies. Publicly, they claim they are doing it only to find candidates for clinical trials; privately, it is not known what other uses of data they make. We do know that Blue Chip Marketing used data about people's premium cable TV and fast-food consumption to pinpoint people to target for advertisements for an obesity study and that a company called Acurian used data indicating a love for jazz music, cat ownership, and sweepstakes entries to find patients for an arthritis study.[16] Companies admit cold-calling patients on the basis of this data and asking if they'd like to participate in an obesity or arthritis study, respectively.

Similarly, insurers and employers have used Facebook to disprove workers' compensation claims. For example, one Arkansas man was denied benefits when photos of his drinking and partying after allegedly suffering a debilitating back injury were unearthed,[17] and a California woman was convicted of workers' compensation fraud after she typed more than two hundred posts (not terribly clever) to Facebook after claiming that a wrist injury prevented her from typing at work.[18]

Of course, this kind of scoring gets even more scary when the data is processed automatically and across millions of records. For example, insurers Allfinanz and TCP LifeSystems are trying to automate a process for predicting your longevity before they issue an insurance policy by analyzing all kinds of detailed data, down to whether you pay bills by ATM or by check (apparently, ATM users live longer than check writers; who knows why).[19] As the amount of data available grows, more and more scores like this will be issued—and more companies will routinely grant or deny benefits on the basis of it.

Reputation Scoring 2.0

One easy way to understand how sophisticated computer scoring has become is to compare early search engines to the complex algorithms currently used by Google, Bing, or any other current search engine. We all know that when we type something into Google's search box—let's say the words *Reputation Economy*—Google calculates a score for all the pages on the Internet that contain the words *Reputation Economy*. Pages with higher scores are shown at the top of the search results, and pages with lower scores are shown at the bottom.

The thing is, this score is based not only on objective facts but also on how those facts are calculated and weighted by the computer, and the weight that each fact is given is just as important as the facts themselves. For example, back in the mid-1990s, early search engines like AltaVista simply added up the number of times a word appeared on a given Web page and used that to create a quality score for that Web page. For example, pages on which the phrase *Reputation Economy* was repeated frequently would get a high score and thus show up at the top of a list of search results for the title of this book. This led to obvious problems with spam: page owners could just repeat a word over and over at the bottom of the screen in hope of deceiving the search engines (it was never terribly effective as a strategy and it's entirely useless today, but that didn't stop a lot of people from trying). The way the facts were weighted created very strong incentives for bad behavior and failed to reward good content.

But in 1996 scoring changed forever when two Stanford Ph.D. students named Sergey Brin and Larry Page created a new way to assign scores to Web pages. Instead of just counting the times that certain words occurred, their algorithm (which eventually became the first Google search engine) effectively counted links to Web pages as "votes" for the importance of a page. If one hundred Web pages (at the time, a lot) all linked to the home page of IBM.com, for example, then that home page might get a score of 100, which was then turned into a PageRank of 10. Then, when a user typed in a Web search for "IBM," the algorithm would factor in *both* the popularity of the page at IBM.com *and* how often that page used the term *IBM* when serving up its search results. Brin and Page set up a test system in a Stanford dorm room, at first using the domain name "google.stanford.edu" before acquiring the familiar Google.com.

Within months, they realized the power of the system and in-corporated Google.

Over the years, Google's scoring system has evolved to in-clude many other factors and data points. The details of today's system are closely guarded secrets, but the point is that each score is based on a whole host of dizzyingly complex and yet in-stantaneous mathematical calculations: How many other sites link to this page? What percentage of users click on this result? Is this site affiliated with a ".edu" domain or a ".com" domain? The list goes on and on. The computer doesn't have to rely on a gut feeling or any emotions about how credible or reliable or relevant to the search query the site is; it just follows whatever formula it has been given.

In the same way that Google figured out how to use the mas-sive amount of search data to score Web pages, companies have figured out how to use the massive amounts of personal data to score people, businesses, relationships, and more. The busi-ness review site Yelp.com is a good example of "version 1.0" of this type of reputation scoring. Yelp asks patrons of restaurants, stores, hotels, and virtually any other type of business to submit reviews and give a star rating, from 1 to 5. The site's algorithm then takes these scores, compiles them, weights them on the basis of factors like whether the computer thinks a particular review might be fake or paid, and displays one aggregate score. But Yelp (and its competitors) will surely move into "scoring 2.0" soon: completely personalized scoring in which the score is based not only on characteristics of the thing being measured (i.e., the starred rating) but also on the person doing the mea-suring. In other words, the scores you see will be matched to your personal preferences. For example, if you are an adven-turesome "foodie" and you consistently review authentic local eateries, the score you see for a major chain restaurant (think Olive Garden) will be lower than the ones displayed to users who have previously given a high score to Applebee's Awesome Blossom (for example).

A similar evolution will play out on services like Klout, which use a mathematical analysis of factors like Twitter and Facebook engagement to measure how influential people are. Right now, this is all "scoring 1.0"—everyone sees the same scores. So unsurprisingly, pop culture icons like Justin Bieber tend to score very highly (the Biebs even beat President Obama as the top Klout score for a while).[20] But what if you haven't caught Bieber fever, and none of your friends have either? In a world of "scoring 2.0," when you log into your Klout account, the people who influence *your* peers specifically—who might be politicians, business leaders, athletes, or some other group entirely—are given higher scores than Bieber.

In other words, your popularity and influence among the *people who matter to you* will be scored. Rather than the old one-size-fits-all model, the future will judge you within your group of peers: Are you the most influential or popular marketing director at ABC Corporation? Are you a leader among nearby distribution warehouse managers? Would you be a good candidate for your leading competitor to recruit with a lucrative bonus and relocation package? These questions—not silly national popularity contests—will be the future of reputation scoring.

So to capitalize on this trend of personalized scoring, what should you do? First, know your market. Think about the people you'd like to be known for influencing, and ruthlessly target them in your public persona. If this sounds false or inauthentic, consider that some of the best leaders are known for their carefully cultivated public personas and images (What is Richard

Branson without his intentionally over-the-top lifestyle? Mark Cuban without controversy? Howard Schultz without social commentary?). So cut *needlessly* personal statements and focus on delivering valuable insights a computer would recognize as consistent with how you want to be perceived by important people in your field.

Even Your Friends Will Be Scored

They say that no man is an island. The phrase may have originally referred to the need for human companionship, but it is also an apt description of the next generation of reputation scoring. In the looming Reputation Economy not only are you being scored on your own behavior, but also your friends, peers, and colleagues will be evaluated when *you* seek a loan, health insurance, or even a job. Hang out with the "right" crowd and you'll be rated more highly, but if the algorithm thinks your friends are a bad influence then certain perks and opportunities won't be available to you.

Companies that do reputation scoring aren't actually crazy to consider the impact of peers. In fact, studies have found that your friends can powerfully influence everything from your spending behavior to your political leanings and even your health. When the Framingham Heart Study analyzed thirty years of health records of more than five thousand residents of the town of Framingham, Massachusetts, one shocking finding was that if a subject became obese the chance that his friends would also become obese more than doubled.[21] The study not only has become part of the canon of community health intervention but also has been applied equally by the purveyors of insurance products: given the choice, no life insurer would sell a top-tier policy to someone whose best friend had just gained fifty pounds.

Other studies are still relatively nascent, but early results suggest that unwanted behaviors like defaulting on loans may be similarly contagious. After all, it doesn't take a Ph.D. to figure out that friends often share similar values, consumer preferences, spending habits, and more; in the world of Big Analysis it is not unreasonable to assume that the data scientists will discover other methods for predicting our future behavior on the basis of the past behavior of our friends and cohorts.

Scarier still, as the Reputation Economy develops, these reputation scores will no longer be the private property or sole purview of the companies that compile them; soon they will be made publicly available and searchable to everyone. Indeed, the natural culmination of all these trends is a "reputation engine," similar to a search engine, except that instead of searching for Web pages with relevant information about a particular topic, reputation engines will search the massive databases of personal information to return all of the relevant information about a person—or find a person who meets a set of criteria. Just as search engines were the trend of the first decade of the 2000s, reputation engines will be the trend of the next decade. And in fact, early reputation engines already exist: for example, when you search for a person on the site Spokeo.com, it will show you a *wealth score* for that person in addition to demographic information. The short-lived Honestly.com allowed anyone to search aggregated anonymous comments about people's work performance. Newsle.com aggregates news references to your Facebook friends and publishes them on its website and in a newsletter automatically sent to subscribers' inboxes. (Want to know every time any of your Facebook friends is in the "real" news? Easy enough—for better or worse.) Klout and Kred, which score people's influence on social media, make those Newsle.com scores open to the public.

And the next generation of reputation engines will go further, aggregating all of this information into one easy-to-use interface. We jokingly call this the "I know what you did last summer" engine—an as-yet hypothetical website that anyone can log into and see all of the activity of friends (and crushes and exes and so forth) across the Internet. Pieces of this have already surfaced: the site Face.com allowed you to search for untagged photos of your friends until Facebook bought it and shut it down, the start-up Ark.com advertises itself as a way to "discover *everything* about your contacts" by merging information pulled from different social networks plus open search, and Spokeo.com has long been a public interface for government records and huge address databases. All that's missing is one site to merge these concepts into one—and rest assured that it will happen soon enough. The human craving for trading gossip and being in the know will ensure that this becomes a dirty reality.

While it is quite reasonable not to want everything you do to be factored into some score that will haunt you for eternity, don't bother trying to avoid it entirely; there's no way to "live off the grid" online. Forget just trying to "hide" your photos and posts on Facebook; the reputation engines of the future won't have an easy opt-out mechanism, and we will all participate whether we like it or not. Even if you don't have a Facebook account, your friends will, and anything they post about you— even photos in which you are not specifically tagged—are fair game for reputation scoring (remember, Facebook bought the facial recognition company Face.com). And even if you delete your browsing history and make all your purchases securely, your electronic transactions and Web browsing history will still be recorded and tallied. True, there are some ways to reduce the amount of data that is collected—you can opt out of some online tracking cookies, and you can set a "do not track" request in your browser—but those ways are not foolproof, so don't be lulled into a false sense of security just by taking those measures.

In fact, intentionally deleting part of your online history (like deleting your Facebook or Twitter account) may be viewed as a negative sign and may actually lower your scores on measures like trustworthiness and credibility. For one thing, an increasing number of services like Airbnb (peer-to-peer vacation and short-term housing rentals) and Nexon (online gaming) look up your Facebook account to verify that you are a real person; if they come up empty, they will assume you are a scammer or a spammer, and your access may be denied. Others—particularly an increasing number that rely on social trust, like peer-to-peer car rental and house sharing—use your Facebook or LinkedIn account not only to loosely verify your identity but also to make the implied threat of damaging your reputation in case of misconduct (for example, by posting on your wall that you trashed a host's apartment). Similarly, even if you don't want to tweet a steady lifestream ("eating hamburgers #yummytummy"), simply having a long-established Twitter account can serve as a positive input to algorithms that seek to uncover your online history.

Plus, computers don't like uncertainty, and scoring algorithms are likely programmed to draw certain inferences if your footprint is missing data that most other people's footprints have: Was this area of your life intentionally wiped out to delete something bad, like a bankruptcy, a long period of unemployment, or worse? So long as most people in your professional sphere continue to use Facebook, LinkedIn, Web-based e-mail, and other services, anyone who doesn't will stand out— and probably for the wrong reasons. Take the example of one German newspaper that noted that two recent mass murderers had opted out of online social life and went on to suggest that anyone who avoided Facebook and other online tools might be suspicious.[22] Yes, it's an unfair inference, but it's one that will probably be drawn whether you like it or not.

With the growth of facial recognition, license plate scanners, and other technologies that you can't realistically avoid (covering one's license plate is generally illegal, and don't try walking into a bank with your face covered for anything other than religious reasons), it's safe to assume that anything you do on or offline is being stored and scored.

So instead of trying to hide negative information from the computers and their scoring algorithms, the best strategy is to carefully curate your digital footprint so that the *positive* information will eclipse and counterbalance all the negative data that you don't have control over. Luckily, there are some tricks and techniques you can employ to boost that positive information in ways that will improve your scores.

First, remember that since your scorer is, after all, a computer, it is crucial that any positive information about you be recorded and stored in a way that a computer understands. If it can't be quantified and scored, in other words, it doesn't count. That doesn't mean that everything you do needs to be just a number; computers are becoming increasingly skilled at picking out meaning from text. But it does mean that the more tangible and easy-to-quantify accomplishments (like graduating with a 4.0, increasing company sales in your region by 5 percent, decreasing employee turnover by 20 percent, or donating to ten charities) are far more convincing to a computer, and thus more likely to bump up your reputation scores, than accomplishments that are harder to quantify or verify, like taking a noncredit course, creating a sense of ownership in the company, helping a junior employee in another department boost his or her sales performance, or giving change to a homeless person, even if the latter may be more important in the long run.

To be clear, we're not advocating that you give up on important goals just to focus on short-term self-promotion; if creating a sense of ownership among employees is important to your business, then you should do it. The point is simply to make sure that computers see the tangible accomplishments in addition to the intangible ones and to be sure that these accomplishments are in a digital, searchable, storable form—for example, a picture of you with the winning team is useless without a caption citing your name and the team's accomplishment. By carefully curating and highlighting positive information—successes at work, trust among friends, a positive social life, and more—you can flood the computers and scoring systems with the type of information you prefer. That doesn't mean you should get on Facebook and brag about every trip to the gym and every memo successfully drafted—and, frankly, nobody cares about your seven-minute mile, your seventeenth trip to CrossFit this month (or how many burpees you did), or even whether you nailed your TPS reports. But a steady stream of healthy social interactions, photos, and positive comments creates the sort of stream that the computers are looking for.

Similarly, and this one should be obvious, avoid putting negative content online. Posting on Facebook (or, worse, your publicly accessible blog) may be a good way to vent about getting fired or dumped from a relationship—but it also creates a permanent record of the event and your response to it. At a minimum, secure those sorts of posts with the highest possible privacy settings so that only your friends can see them. Or, better yet, pick up the phone and call your friends; so far, no private database companies have been caught listening in on phone calls.

On the professional side, populate and update your LinkedIn and similar professional networking pages with a steady stream of projects and responsibilities. There's no need to go over the top; most jobs don't need an update every week or even every month. But after major milestones it's worth sending an update. Similarly for very public sites, like Twitter and other social networks or sharing services, try to connect to or follow at least a few influential people in your industry; ideally you want to be connected with a mix of leaders in your company and show mutual engagement with people important in your field—for example, by commenting on each other's blog posts or retweeting one another's tweets. If you hit a major milestone at work, tweet about it. Even better, be humble and give credit to your colleagues for their hard work: doing so makes you look appreciative and still associates you with the positive outcome.

In fact, making them look better (such as by giving them public kudos for a team accomplishment) will make you score better too. And your colleagues will be more likely to repay the favor and thank you for your contribution if you establish a culture of mutual public recognition. As just a trivial example of a self-reinforcing cycle of positive recognition, many LinkedIn users have found that endorsing their peers and colleagues leads to a significant number of mutual endorsements without any prompting at all. Multiply that by a variety of feedback mechanisms (Twitter, LinkedIn, Facebook, blogs, etc.) and the effect can become very powerful.

And keep in mind that there will be plenty of useful and socially positive ways to use reputation engines too—imagine searching for a babysitter and being able to know with confidence whether the person is kind, responsible, and trustworthy. Or imagine looking for a loan or investment for your business and being able to tell whether a potential partner is financially solvent, has good judgment, and has displayed integrity in previous transactions. So try to use information out there about *other* people's reputation to your advantage when you can.

In short, reputation scores are like currency: score well and you'll be flush with opportunities, score poorly and doors will slam closed. Over the next several chapters, we'll discuss more specific ways you can become reputation rich in a world where everything about you is being recorded, analyzed, and scored.

Potent

Don't Stop Believing
(in the Power of Reputation
to Shape Your Career)

REPUTATION HAS SUCH A POTENT EFFECT ON OUR CA-
reers, it can make literal rock stars out of unknowns
virtually overnight. In February 2007, Arnel Pineda was
a small-time singer based in Manila, the Philippines. He had
spent two years homeless before becoming a singer for a variety of local bands, playing mostly in the Philippines with occa-
sional stints in nearby Hong Kong. He had found stability, but
not commercial success, as part of a local band called the Zoo.
The Zoo played local bars and restaurants like the Bagaberde
in Manila (capacity three hundred) and the Hard Rock Cafe,
Makati (capacity five hundred), and had one minimally successful album to its name.

By February 2008, Pineda's life had changed. That month, Pineda embarked on a world tour as the new front man of the American rock band Journey, playing sold-out concerts worldwide. His first show with Journey was at a music festival in Chile (capacity twenty thousand), which was quickly followed by a tour of sold-out outdoor venues across the United States. By the end of 2008, Pineda had played fifty-seven shows to over one million fans. In early 2009, the tour even returned to Manila, where, thanks to the strength of the hometown welcome, Journey and Pineda recorded a live album before a crowd of thirty thousand fans at the Mall of Asia Concert Grounds.

How did Pineda make the leap from local bars in the Philippines to leading the group that *USA Today* called the "fifth best American rock band of all time" (whose anthem "Don't Stop Believing" is the #1 most downloaded classic rock song on iTunes of all time, with well over two million downloads)? In short, a very basic form of digital reputation.

In 2006 and 2007, Pineda (with help from a bandmate) uploaded to YouTube his own cover versions of classic rock standards from bands like Aerosmith, Air Supply, the Eagles, Kenny Loggins, and Journey. His covers never went "viral" (in the sense of achieving millions of views seemingly overnight); unlike 2012's surprise viral hit "Gangnam Style," his videos attracted thousands rather than millions of viewers. But his listeners were consistently impressed: many clicked the "thumbs up" button and clicked from one of his videos to another. For example, viewers of Pineda's cover of Journey's ballad "Faithfully" gave it more than seventy "thumbs up" votes for every one "thumbs down."[1]

YouTube's automatic computer ranking system interpreted these "thumbs up" votes and the loyalty of his viewers as evidence of the quality of the videos. Of course, the computer didn't know who Pineda was, or even whether he was a good singer; all it knew was that thousands of viewers were clicking on Pineda's songs and liking them. To the system, this meant "high quality," which signaled its algorithm to rank these highly supported videos closer to the top of search results, thus creating a new wave of viewers who could easily stumble on and give a "thumbs up" to his best videos. Over time, Pineda's videos began to appear higher and higher on the results for searches such as "Faithfully cover" and "Journey cover."

Of course, appearing at the top of YouTube search results is no guarantee of overnight celebrity; if it were, thousands of cats with laser pointers would be hosting their own TV shows. Instead, it took an unusual search for Pineda to have his moment in the sun.

In mid-2007, Neal Schon, a guitarist and the most consistent member of Journey, was searching for a new lead singer for the band. The band's original singer, Steve Perry, had moved on to solo projects years ago. One replacement, Steve Augeri, was dropped when a medical ailment destroyed his singing voice. The band then tried Jeff Scott Soto, but he too was quickly dropped, for unexplained reasons. Nostalgia for the 1980s was running high, but the band couldn't tour without a lead singer.

After traditional searches failed, Neal Schon tried searching YouTube for potential candidates to fill the gap. The exact search term Schon used is lost to history, but whatever it was, the video of Pineda and the Zoo covering Journey's "Faithfully" appeared near the top of the results page.

Schon had never heard of the Zoo or Pineda, but he was impressed by the quality of the singing he heard: even though it was midnight when he found Pineda's video, he immediately called Journey's keyboardist Jonathan Cain and told him he'd found "the one": Schon told Cain to watch the "Faithfully" video "right now, go to the computer! Go!"[2] As Schon put it, "After watching the videos over and over again, I had to walk away from the computer and let what I heard sink in because it sounded too good to be true. I thought, 'he can't be that good.' But he is that good, he's the real deal."[3]

Schon then e-mailed Pineda to ask if he were interested in auditioning to sing with Journey. Pineda, jaded after years in the industry, thought an e-mail claiming to be from Neal Schon (let alone asking him to consider *joining* Journey) was a hoax and almost didn't respond. But Pineda eventually answered, and he was on a plane to California within days. Pineda wasn't the only one skeptical that an unknown YouTube phenomenon could really get an interview with a legendary rock band: when Pineda applied for a visa, the U.S. Citizenship and Immigration Services initially found this this story so improbable that Pineda had to sing Journey's hit "Wheel in the Sky" in order to convince the immigrations officer that he really was going to California to audition for a job with Journey.[4] Apparently, his singing was convincing enough; he got the visa he needed and was allowed into the United States.

Pineda spent two days auditioning with Journey in Marin County, California, before being offered the opportunity to tour as Journey's new lead singer. The rest of the story is just fodder for *Behind the Music*: millions of dollars, stadium tours, screaming fans, groupies, and all the rest that comes with being a rock star.

As our Reputation Economy matures, digital reputation will profoundly change the way talent is discovered. And not just for rock stars; computer-aided reputation screening is rapidly transforming the ways in which employees of all stripes are recruited, hired, promoted, demoted, and fired. The previous chapters showed why digital reputation will become an indelible, potent, always-on global force. This chapter will show how reputation—particularly the kind of reputation that can be digitized and used by computers in a hybrid decision-making process with humans—will affect almost every individual's career trajectory and will discuss how to optimize your digital footprint to accelerate yours.

Decisions Almost Made by Machine

As computers have become more powerful and as digital information about individuals' reputations has become more plentiful, computers are making an increasing number of important decisions that were formerly made by humans in areas ranging from hiring to firing to promoting to punishing. We call this trend "decisions almost made by machine" (and the process getting "DAMMed"). The term at least captures the core idea: computers are being charged with making decisions with minimal human oversight. As the Reputation Economy matures, decisions about increasingly important subjects will be largely entrusted to computers—glitches and all—and an increasingly large portion of our interactions will be directed by computers with little or no possible appeal to human common sense.

The growth of DAMM will not completely separate humans from decision making. After all, it's "decisions *almost* made by machine." Sometimes humans will be involved, but not until the last step of a process—such as making the final choice as to which candidate to hire or which employee to let go—by which point the computer has already shaped the outcome by preselecting which candidates are even up for consideration, or by gently pushing candidates forward or backward through the course of their careers.

Take our Journey example. It's true that Neal Schon made

the final decision to invite Arnel Pineda to California for an in-person audition, and the band as a whole decided to invite Pineda to tour with them. But it was a form of DAMM that put Pineda in the position to get the opportunity at all: when Neal Schon searched YouTube, a computer at YouTube's server farm sorted through thousands of covers of Journey songs and placed one of Pineda's among the most relevant search results to put on the first page. The YouTube system heavily influenced Schon's ultimate choice by ranking Pineda's version over the versions of hundreds of other potential candidates. In fact, it's unlikely that Schon ever made it past the first few pages of YouTube search results; had YouTube's system displayed search results in some other order (or even just random order), Schon would have never even seen Pineda's haunting cover of "Faithfully," and Pineda would probably still be playing bars and clubs around Manila. Maybe if YouTube were using a different algorithm, Journey would have its first female lead singer—or maybe Schon would never have found a candidate and would have given up in frustration. Either way, the computer was just as in control of the process as Schon, powering Pineda's ascension to the world of rock stardom. It's the perfect example of a decision almost made by machine.

In this chapter we'll see how sometimes, if you have a good reputation, DAMM can create a sudden leap in your career, and how other times it can be like a steady breeze pushing you in the direction you want to go. If you have a bad reputation, however, DAMM can act like a stiff headwind, pushing you away from your goals. No matter what, DAMM and digital reputation will have an increasingly powerful impact on your career as the Reputation Economy continues to grow. Once you gain an understanding of how it works, you'll learn how you can use it to propel your own career forward.

A Sudden Jump Forward

It is impossible to overestimate the power of reputation for your career, especially in a world of decisions all but made by machine. One of the most powerful and direct ways that digital reputation has begun to affect individuals is in the hiring process: computer-driven screening is now largely determining which candidates get which jobs. And it's easy to see why.

Computers present an attractive—if not downright tempting—way to take the pain out of these hiring decisions. Hiring managers and human recruiters are slow and expensive, whereas computers can analyze thousands of decisions each second, don't take breaks, never get bored, and don't demand a weekly paycheck. Well-meaning organizations and companies have already entrusted computers with thousands of decisions formerly made by humans, and all evidence suggests that the trend will continue as computers continue to become cheaper and more ubiquitous.

The sheer number of applications received for many positions makes computer processing all but a necessity. Consider the Mars One organization, a nonprofit foundation set up with the goal of funding the first one-way manned mission to Mars. It received over *200,000* applications to be an astronaut on a mission that might never happen (the organization remains approximately $5.7 billion short of what it estimates to be a total cost of $6 billion).[5] Even if a human were to spend just five minutes per application, it would take a reviewer nine years working full time just to process all of the applications received. And even that is small by private sector standards; Walmart receives *5 million* applications per year.[6] There are other reasons that computer-automated screening is attractive to employers. In addition to improving and speeding the hiring process, it can also help reduce or even eliminate the element of bias in the hiring process, which can alone potentially save a company millions of dollars in lawsuits and lawyers' fees.

The problem of discrimination in the hiring process is widespread enough; it has even attracted copious attention from academic researchers. In 2001, a pair of scholars from the University of Chicago and MIT set out to test employment practices at large U.S. companies. They tried a simple experiment: in response to 1,300 real "help wanted" advertisements, they sent more than five thousand fake résumés. On half of the résumés, they placed names that were statistically more common among white households ("Emily Walsh"), and on the other half they placed names that were statistically more common among black households ("Lakisha Washington").[7] Other than the names, the résumés were calibrated to show equal work experience and skill levels. The results have become part of the employment discrimination canon: despite companies' promises of race-neutral hiring, the "white" résumés received callbacks 9.65 percent of the time, but the "black" résumés received callbacks just 6.45 percent of the time.

Computer automation is a tempting way to solve this first layer of discrimination by insulating the process from humans. Unless somebody tells it, a computer doesn't know any difference between "Emily Walsh" and "Lakisha Washington." As a result, the first step of automation is already in place at many large companies: employment applications are automatically scanned by computer to search for certain minimum requirements, such as having a college degree or an equivalent credential, or listing at least one prior job. The final hiring decision may still be made by a human, but hundreds (or thousands) of résumés are eliminated before a human ever sees them. If your résumé is among those that a computer automatically eliminates, it doesn't matter how impressive you might be in person; you'll never get a chance to make that first impression.

Successful candidates are beating the screeners by preparing their résumés and application materials in a way that makes it easy for a computer to recognize and categorize their accomplishments. And as we'll discuss in this chapter and the next, the tricks smart candidates are using are applicable to more than just getting your foot in the door: they are a foundation for any job application in a DAMM world. The goal is to make sure that a computer—with no ability to recognize indirect references— can easily determine (a) that your application displays at least the minimum qualifications for the job and (b) that it displays all the characteristics that their algorithms are looking for.

These trends are well under way. Companies like S2Verify sell services to employers that automatically classify hundreds or even thousands of incoming résumés as "not eligible" or "eligible" on the basis of keyword lists provided by the employer. These keywords might be as simple as verifying that *college* or *university* appears on a résumé (sorry, graduates of the London School of Economics) or as complex as screening for particular skills not mentioned in the ad itself (looking for a job in early childhood education? Better have your qualifications in language development itemized even if not asked for). If the old advice for job seeking was to use action verbs in your résumé as much as possible ("*Led* team to *transform* supply chain . . ."), the new advice is to add enough keywords about your function, role, and technologies to make sure that even the worst computer screener will pick it up ("Led *procurement* team to transform *purchasing, receiving, and distribution* technologies of *supply chain*").

How do these keyword services work? The employer sends all résumés received to a résumé-screening service provider or buys software that does the same thing internally. The computer then looks for keywords based on the employer's requirements: for example, the computer might scan for at least two years of total job history in any field involving "retail" or any synonym of *retail*. The résumé-scanning company then sends back a list of eligible résumés so that the hiring manager has to look through only maybe thirty résumés instead of three thousand.

In some ways, this service is not very different from the work of many human first-line hiring managers, who also quickly sort through many résumés on the basis of a required minimum level of experience. But, as prepared candidates have discovered, the process of optimizing a résumé for a computer scanning service is very different from optimizing for a human reader. Computers are tremendously literal and (at least for now) struggle to grasp subtle shades of meaning. If a job advertisement calls for "CPA," it's a good bet that somebody programmed the screening software to search for résumés that have the word *accounting* in them. Unfortunately, the screen might be programmed by somebody who doesn't know to look for less obvious keywords, like perhaps *bookkeeper* or maybe even *comptroller* as signals of relevant experience (you can forget *finance ninja*—you may laugh, but no shortage of early 2010s job descriptions in San Francisco called for "____ ninjas," where the blank was filled in by everything from *engineering* through *espresso*). Given that résumés with the "right" keywords will advance to the next stage while others will advance to the trash bin, you should help the system by subtly inserting synonyms and related terms where you can. And don't get cute: even if you know that both you and the hiring manager went to Stanford, don't list it as "the Farm" (a nickname not widely known outside the Bay Area), lest the computer think you're a cowpoke rather than a Pac-12 grad (same for "the U" for any Miami University Hurricanes, or any other similar insider nicknames that might be well-known among humans but will register as duds to a computer).

Some automated résumé-screening services go even further and integrate basic information from background checks, such as criminal convictions, prior employers, and credit scores. Employers can ask their screening computer system to automatically reject all ex-felons (or, if state law allows, all criminal convictions generally) or even to eliminate candidates who omitted prior employers. Sometimes this is based on employment checks; other times it's based on a long gap between jobs—so if you have a gaping hole in your résumé, make sure you fill it, even if just to say you were freelancing or self-employed. Some programs even filter out people who have had recent bankruptcies (a controversial practice, but one commonly used for positions that require handling large amounts of cash).

More advanced systems are beginning to look for more than just keywords that suggest certain qualifications or experience: they are looking for hints to the *quality* of experience. For example, in many jobs your career *growth* is more important than your current *position*. So smart algorithms are starting to learn the difference between a candidate who has stagnated and a candidate who has worked her way up. In these advanced systems, having *mail room* in your résumé is a virtue, not a liability, because it shows that you worked your way up (unless, of course, you still work in the mail room). So when describing your job history, make sure there's a clear path from lesser to greater responsibility that a computer can pick up on. And be sure to emphasize your career growth in quantifiable ways—whether in the size of the organization, the size of the budget, the number of direct reports, or whatever other objective measurement a computer might understand.

Being at a company during a growth phase may also be more beneficial than being there during a fall, especially if your department or role (such as marketing, sales, or engineering) may have been directly responsible for that growth (compared to, say, finance)—highlight those unique experiences. Personalize your résumé for your target: if you're applying for a consulting position, emphasize how many different companies you've worked for and industries you've serviced; if you're applying for a traditional firm where the average employee tenure is more than ten years, focus on stability and a limited set of your past.

As we've seen, sometimes the role of DAMM can be dramatic: a high-profile bandmate plucked from the masses by computer-aided selection. Other times, it can be pedestrian: a large pool of entry-level candidates narrowed by computer. And sometimes it can drive important decisions that are finished by humans: one résumé is placed at the top of the stack on the basis of keywords matching an analysis. But no matter how it is implemented, the impact on candidates can be significant: a new job opportunity granted or denied on the basis of the way a computer ranked you among hundreds or thousands of people.

That said, in a world of DAMM, humans often still have the final say. A résumé filled with nothing but keywords might pass the automated screeners but would be unlikely to pass the final human review. Just as e-mail spam is often easily recognized by human e-mail readers, résumé spam stands out to human reviewers. The point is that a résumé containing interesting content but no relevant keywords will probably never get a chance to make an impression on a human reviewer; the computerized screener is likely to reject the résumé even if the candidate would be the perfect fit.

How to Beat the Machine

Pineda's story illustrates three principles of succeeding in the DAMM world. Whether deliberately or not, he demonstrated how an individual can leverage DAMM to land a dream job.

First, Pineda *cast a wide net* in his search. When he put his videos on YouTube, he targeted a global audience. He didn't necessarily plan to get a job in the United States when he started posting videos—after all, most of his work was in the Philippines and Hong Kong—but he still put his work out as publicly as possible. As a result, many potential employers and partners could find him and see a sample of his work.

Second, he *publicized himself in a way that was honest and authentic and appropriate* given his current job: he posted videos of himself performing with his bandmates and promoted the band just as much as he promoted his own career. It appeared that he was the standout star of the band, but that's only because he actually *was* the star of the band; he didn't try to fake it or present himself as something he wasn't.

Finally, Pineda *was prepared to act when opportunity knocked*. Pineda was born with huge natural talent, but he spent many years practicing his singing and building a stage presence by working the Philippine bar circuit. When he got a chance to interview with Journey, it was a job he'd spent his life unknowingly preparing for. When he realized that the interview with Journey was real (and not a hoax), he dropped everything he was doing and flew to California for the interview. To take the words of another author, he was ready for a so-called black swan—an unexpected event that he could never foresee. There is no way he could have known that Journey would come calling, or when he would receive his big break, but he had prepared himself for it by staying sharp and promoting himself widely. Consider the impact if Pineda had gotten complacent and stopped practicing; if the twelve-hour flight from San Francisco to Manila seems long, just imagine how long it would feel to Pineda if he had to ride it home knowing that he'd missed the chance of a lifetime because he'd let his voice get rusty. When Pineda started posting his videos on YouTube, he had no idea that he was going to be given an opportunity to go on a world-wide tour, but he accepted the surprise when it came—with open arms.

The Power of DAMM as a Steady Breeze

The impact of digital reputation and DAMM decisions don't get much more powerful than turning somebody into a rock star almost overnight. But the right kind of reputation and DAMM can also give you steady, if less dramatic, nudges that add up over time. Think of it as a gentle breeze at your back, pushing you in the direction you want to go. (Or it can work the other way with a bad digital reputation.)

Truth be told, very few people will ever get a million-dollar opportunity to tour with a world-famous band. By the same token, few people will get a cold call from a recruiter offering them a CEO post. Instead, much of the power of a good reputation in the Reputation Economy will take the form of hundreds of small opportunities being available to the best-prepared job seekers and career climbers. People who can optimize their reputation to take advantage of a DAMM world will be presented with opportunities that seem small or even insignificant at the time. But those who take advantage of the small opportunities will find that progressively larger opportunities follow. In turn, taking those larger opportunities can create even more opportunities down the road, creating a virtuous cycle propelling you toward your goals.

To take one example of how a series of subtle pushes can add up, consider the process of how a CEO of a major public company (like IBM or Google) is chosen. We're a long way away from a computer unilaterally appointing the next CEO of a public company—in fact, it's unlikely to happen during the authors' lifetimes. But the influence of DAMM will still be a significant factor in who is chosen. Long before the CEO is picked, the top candidate (let's call her Alice) has already been groomed for the job: she has been selected for training opportunities, selected to attend key conferences, and given management-track promotions within the organization. By contrast, another would-be candidate (let's call him Bob) was passed over for a key management training initiative (which led to future offsite training events and networking meetings), so his résumé looks incomplete by comparison. It's hard to overestimate the power of DAMM in these situations; even if it is unlikely that a computer would make the final selection of Alice as CEO, by the time she is up for the job, she has already been blessed with all the experiences that add up to the perfect résumé—she's the only choice, really. If a computer selects people for internal training and promotion (and computers will do so), the computer can shape the choice of the person who is ready for the next step.

How do computers pick Alice from among thousands of junior and midlevel employees for opportunities available only to a few? While a *Hunger Games* model comes to mind, in reality it works just like consumer scoring models: computer algorithms compare thousands of variables to make predictions about people. Instead of looking at consumer characteristics (e.g., in general, are people who listen to Nickelback good or bad customers?), employment scoring models use employment-related data: Who shows up consistently and stays late—but not too late (desperation, an affair, or an inability to manage time)? Who works on teams that consistently succeed? Whose e-mail correspondence is consistent with making friends "up" the corporate hierarchy? Whose e-mails start "flame wars" and distracting bickering sessions in the office? Who follows most of the rules (but not quite all of them—those people aren't independent enough thinkers) in her job? Who has not made any indication of jumping ship such as constantly browsing LinkedIn (except in sales roles, which might call for *more* usage)?

In some ways, this computer-guided selection is better than the old games of office politics where getting selected for opportunities depended on working for the right boss at the right time when Alice would have had the right amount of political influence in the organization. But in other ways, the computers may be just as flawed; here, the computer stacked the deck in Alice's favor (and against Bob) long before the humans got around to picking between the two, possibly on the basis of flawed assumptions about which of the two would make best person for the job.

In this way, digital reputation can add up over time. In the short run a computer's decision to select Alice over Bob to attend one training session can be a very small difference between their careers; it will seem to be a minor disappointment at best (if Bob is even aware that he has missed out). But over a series of these decisions Alice's résumé can end up entirely different from Bob's, all because of a series of small nudges from a computer. Of course, the process of becoming a CEO, a professional athlete, a famous artist, or a successful entrepreneur (or nearly anything else that represents the apogee of a career) requires a combination of aptitude and hundreds of little opportunities added up over time.

From the outside, it looks as if some people are just always in the right place at the right time. But, in reality, being in the right place at the right time is often based on years of hard work building and cultivating a reputation, and hundreds of small decisions (increasingly made by computers) that add up to a big opportunity. Despite what the movies would have you believe, it's relatively unheard of for the coach to pull a weekend warrior out of the stands and put her in for the big game; likewise, it's still rare to pull an employee into a management position without significant training. Similarly, inexperienced managers are not promoted to CEO without gaining significant experience and luck. The story of Pineda making the leap from YouTube is so rare as to make it memorable (although in chapter 5 we will discuss how self-made celebrities can use their reputation to get themselves hired several levels above where their job history would seem to suggest, sometimes with unseemly large bonuses), but most "overnight" artistic successes are the result of years (if not decades) of work.

Stand Out from the Crowd

Don't get us wrong. We aren't completely knocking DAMM. In fact, there are many ways beyond just optimizing your résumé that you can leverage DAMM to your career advantage. For example, consider that today companies are increasingly bemoaning how difficult it is to find talent even from among large pools of applicants. If you've ever had to hire someone for a job, you've probably had the experience yourself: thousands of résumés, yet not one candidate with the right skills, experience, and disposition. As a result, hiring managers and recruiters are being increasingly proactive in looking for and luring great candidates. In other words, whether you're aware of it or not, there might be some recruiter out there searching for someone to do exactly the job *you* want—even when no job is posted. So how can *you* attract the attention of these recruiters in the world of DAMM?

First, become a broadcaster. Get your content out into the world and into the hands of reputation engines that will be crawling the Internet at all times looking for material. We're not saying that you should tweet every fifteen minutes—and especially not launch a flood of trivialities. Nor should you bombard Facebook with posts—quite frankly, your privacy is still worth trying to preserve, and there's no reason to make your friends suffer through hundreds of your PowerPoint slides. But by making smart comments, sharing interesting articles, and engaging with others in your field online in respectful, intelligent conversation, you can demonstrate to the world that you are professional and on top of the trends and milestones in your field. Even just being connected to influencers and thought leaders can give a positive shine to your image—and will certainly help others find you.

Next, hang your digital shingle. Once you've been found, your search results will be treated like your digital résumé. In fact, the authors have each found jobs without ever writing a formal résumé, solely on the basis of their search results—and we are hardly alone. Thanks to the continuous and real-time nature of digital search, you're in constant, unwitting job application mode without even trying.

Establish refreshable digital profiles across all your online properties. For example, buy your own domain name and update it with professional content about yourself, start an industry-related blog and post frequently about the latest breaking developments or trends, keep your LinkedIn profile comprehensive and current, and be an early adopter of whatever other professional services become popular over the next few years. You don't have to be a technology expert: plenty of point-and-click services exist for each of these tasks. Make sure your content is fresh and updated regularly—it doesn't have to be every day, but at least once a month and preferably at least weekly.

Not everything you post has to be a work of art—especially if much of it will just be used by computers to see if you're current in your field. Even just posting links (possibly with a sentence or two summary) to articles you've found interesting can be adequate; it shows that you are engaged in your field and reading the trades. If simply posting links seems like an easy way out, remember that the blogging service Tumblr found its initial success in making it very easy for a huge number of people to share and repost content created by others—millions of people signed up, and Tumblr was eventually bought by Yahoo! for $1.1 billion (yes, "billion") for its innovations.

Next, make sure your online and offline worlds are consistent. In the ideal scenario, what's online about you will match who you are in real life. When you tout your passion for classic literature in a job interview, but a quick search turns up your *Fifty Shades of Grey* fan-fic blog—well, that's confusing and could even be off-putting. It's even worse if you claim to love animals but post recipes featuring veal and foie gras. A consistent message will create a positive cycle of reinforcement: what you say offline matches what they find online, and what they find matches what you say. When that loop is closed, people are more likely to comment on and support your content in ways that are consistent with your messaging, making it even stronger. And it should go without saying that the information that's out there about you must be true. Ditch distracting tidbits and remove any exaggerations, even if you didn't put them there.

Be smart about social media. If you have social media accounts, clean them up and lock them down. Delete posts that could be offensive or misconstrued or could otherwise cause consternation—or at least make them visible only to close friends outside your workplace. Use the tools provided by Facebook and other services to "untag" yourself in photos—and search image services like Google Images to see what else may be out there.[8] Most important, if you use Twitter for your personal friends, set that account to private and create a public account that is exclusively professional. That is the account you *want* recruiters to find, so post accordingly—frequently, intelligently, and respectfully. Save the outrage over the latest episode of *The Voice* for your personal feed to your friends only. That said, post at an appropriate pace and time—if you're not posting for work purposes, don't post during work hours, lest your next potential employer ask why you're wasting time on the clock.

Write coherently, but don't worry about writing perfectly: online, the Queen's English is a dying language. You should avoid needless mistakes, but you can do so by writing brief reactions to interesting news and events in your industry rather than by writing long treatises; no one wants to read a ten-thousand-word blog post, and keep Facebook postings no longer than a tweet.

Show growth over time. As mentioned previously, many employers would prefer to see a more junior candidate who shows the ability to grow over a more senior candidate who is stagnating. To many employers (and not to all—you can't be everything to everyone, so optimize for as many positions as you can), a prospect on an upward trajectory will be a smart investment because that candidate may be able to grow into even larger roles over time. When writing, emphasize what you've learned and how you've grown professionally over the years. Of course, if you're the senior candidate up against the whipper-snappers who claim to be the next hot thing, emphasize your judgment, wisdom, and experience as invaluable assets—in addition to recent career growth.

It really all boils down to this: be intelligent about how you appear—explain your unique expertise and value to the world. By this point in life, there is *something* unique you bring to the table—and someday, there's somebody who will need exactly that. Even if on the surface you're one of a hundred people in the same position at your company, there's still a unique combination of background and skills you can bring to bear. Maybe it's "hard" skills, maybe it's a background, or maybe it's just a cultural fit—you are not only a graphic designer but a graphic designer who is self-starting and able to work on deadline in a competitive environment. Identify those unique attributes, and somebody will find you who wants those unique talents and skills.

And remember that just because most people won't see a sudden change in their career prospects doesn't mean that DAMM won't affect them. In the Reputation Economy, companies will increasingly use DAMM to decide whom to hire in countless jobs—ranging from entry level to the highest positions available. And, perhaps more powerfully, as we'll read about in the next chapter, DAMM will shape internal promotion and training decisions that can change the course of a career by giving some people select opportunities for training and advancement—and passing over others, without their even knowing why.

5

Discoverable

Find Your Soup Can

TO MANY, IT SEEMED AS THOUGH ANDY WARHOL BURST onto the pop art stage out of nowhere. But, in fact, he spent years building the reputation that positioned him to succeed. Warhol graduated from the Carnegie Institute of Technology (now the "Carnegie" of Carnegie Mellon) with a degree in commercial art. In 1949, he parlayed his degree into a regular design job drawing illustrations for advertisements in *Glamour* magazine. He spent much of the early 1950s drawing a salary and living a life typical of a commercial artist. But soon Warhol's colorful illustrations of women's shoes in footwear advertisements began to attract attention.[1] In 1952, he met the art director at RCA Records and asked for a job on the basis of his experience with *Glamour*. After making repeated test drawings, he was able to secure a gig designing album artwork and posters. He began to display some of this commercial work in small galleries, continuing to build a reputation within the New York arts community. He was already a prolific self-promoter and consciously parlayed each of these small portfolio pieces into larger and larger opportunities—no success was too small for him to act as though it were the start of his fifteen minutes.

Warhol's first big break within the art community was his first solo show in Los Angeles in 1962, where he exhibited his famous prints of cans of Campbell's Soup and his images of Marilyn Monroe. The show generated buzz within the art world, but it wasn't a commercial success for Warhol; he sold only six Campbell's Soup prints for $100 each. It wasn't until Warhol, through connections developed in tens of small shows around New York, managed to get himself invited as one of six vanguard artists to the 1964 art show *The American Supermarket* that his soup can imagery was picked up by the mass media. Soon, original prints of the soup can were selling for $1,500 at the *Supermarket* show. By 2006, Los Angeles art collector Eli Broad had purchased one at auction for $11,776,000; in 2010, Christie's sold a larger print of a soup can with a can opener for $23,882,500. The point is that, like most successful people, Warhol didn't achieve success overnight. In fact, if it hadn't been for Warhol's constant work to build and utilize his reputation within the art world, he never would have been in a position to exhibit at the *American Supermarket* show, the big "overnight" break that made him one of the most famous and highest-grossing pop artists of all time. We saw in the preceding chapter how the Reputation Economy will empower massive change in the way that people are hired and fired. We read about how, thanks to DAMM, it is becoming faster, cheaper, and easier for companies and employers to spot top talent than ever before. One very positive result is that the rewards for being top talent will actually increase for those few employees with a good reputation—or at least for those who have figured out how to profit from it. This chapter will show you how you can become one of them.

The Six-Figure Hiring Bonus

Very few employees will ever get a significant signing bonus, and fewer still will do it outside the context of a C-level executive position. But small groups of engineers in California and New York have figured out a way to "hack" their reputations to earn six-figure hiring bonuses from major technology companies like Google, Facebook, and even Yahoo!, and their methods are instructive for all of us.

One of the most prominent inefficiencies in the hiring market recently has been the process of hiring top engineers and software designers. A software designer or engineer in the top 1 percent of productivity can be worth millions to an employer, but a mediocre designer or engineer is worth far less—so much less, in fact, that a programmer who writes buggy code might actually be a net drag on the company if the bugs make it into functional software. The problem for companies is that it is very hard to identify the differences among candidates, particularly among recent college graduates. Two students with equal GPAs at the same school are very likely to perform very differently when placed in a real-life work environment.[2] Quite frankly, grades in school have some predictive power for general skill and knowledge, but most liberal arts exams have little to do with the challenges faced in real-world jobs. (Sorry, people who excelled in a liberal arts education; you might still be a success, but it won't be *only* because you have a degree with Latin on it.)

Even more difficult than picking the best programmer from a group of college graduates is identifying good programmers among new candidates who followed nontraditional paths: it is very difficult for hiring managers to compare candidates with radically different experiences—such as serving in the military in lieu of college, taking an apprenticeship or internship instead of a paid position, getting into programming as a second career, and countless other paths. And by the same token it's equally difficult for these candidates to be discovered, let alone to garner the kinds of starting salaries they desire.

The result has been a uniquely Silicon Valley practice that helps companies more easily find top-notch engineers and software designers, while simultaneously providing those sought-after engineers and designers an opportunity to get hired by desirable companies—and collect six-figure starting bonuses along the way. In short, teams of designers create their own small start-up business. Once thousands of customers flock to the business—thanks to a dazzling bit of tech wizardry and some well-placed PR—the founders go showcase their new product to major tech companies like Google, Yahoo!, and Microsoft (plus whatever other companies are hot and have cash to burn). If the engineer work is good enough and the founders are "buzz-worthy" enough, a so-called acqui-hire deal will be struck: the tech giant will buy the start-up and the founders will join the big company as engineers and designers, but their old product will be closed down after a few months. (There are even downside acqui-hires, where a big company buys out a failing business in order to extract a high-quality engineering team that had a good idea but was selling to the wrong market; think of a great team of lawnmower designers working in Nome, Alaska, or a team of sled-dog trainers in Hawaii.)

For example, when Facebook found itself in need of designers for its push toward improved profile pages, it turned to an acqui-hire of Drop.io, a start-up founded by a promising young talent named Sam Lessin. This file-sharing site had already earned itself quite a reputation; it was named one of *Time* magazine's top fifty websites of 2009, and Lessin was named a finalist for *Businessweek*'s 2009 Entrepreneur of the Year.[3] As of 2009, it had "millions" of users (although anonymous usage makes it difficult to know how many were unique). On October 29, 2010, it was acquired by Facebook for Facebook stock worth somewhere between $5 million and $20 million, depending on when you count. By December 15, 2010, however, the main Drop.io service had been shut down entirely. Today, the domain http://drop.io just redirects to Sam Lessin's personal page, where he mentions that he now works at Facebook. Facebook appears to have entirely discarded the original Drop.io product but to have kept the engineering team behind it, effectively turning the creation of Drop.io into a big (and very expensive) job interview. (Perhaps somewhat ironically given his very public acquisition, Mr. Lessin has indirectly touched upon the topic of reputation, proclaiming as his Twitter tagline that "the value of information is inversely related to how public it is.")

The acquisition of a site like Drop.io just for its engineers is not unusual in Silicon Valley. Similarly, Facebook bought Hot Potato in August of 2010 for $10 million in an all-cash deal and also shuttered all of its services by the end of that year. Facebook also bought Beluga in March of 2011 for an undisclosed amount (also likely in the low- to mid-eight-figure range) and shut it down in October of 2011. Google, Yahoo!, and others have all engaged in what they call "talent acquisitions" of similar growth companies, each time keeping the key individuals but throwing out the actual business.

The acqui-hire is a classic Reputation Economy solution for attracting engineering talent. In an acqui-hire, the start-up serves as a portfolio piece more than an actual business; a start-up with a reputation for A+ engineers and designers will reap the benefits of an acqui-hire deal (in some cases, in the millions of dollars), whereas a start-up with a reputation of mediocrity will not.

Of course, identifying and recruiting the most valuable (and thus highly paid) talent is challenging for companies in all industries, not just for tech companies like Google and Microsoft. We know that there is a range of high performers and low performers in almost every corporate position. But most corporate hiring processes do a poor job of identifying which candidates will be high or low performers. In fact, studies show that traditional hiring methods (usually a "gut instinct" evaluation of a résumé and a personality-based interview) often lead to poor hiring decisions. One study showed that, when asked to use a face-to-face interview to pick between two candidates, a group of MBA students (who were about to become managers in their fields) were able to pick the higher-performing candidate just 56 percent of the time; if they'd simply flipped a coin they would have gotten it right almost as frequently and saved the entire interview process.[4] In other words, our gut instincts just aren't that good when it comes to hiring. As a result, much of hiring depends on luck—good candidates are often rejected for the wrong reasons, and bad candidates are incorrectly offered jobs. And this inefficiency doesn't just cost the hiring company money; it also has the auxiliary effect of lowering salaries for everyone. Because of the difficulty in sorting high and low performers, it is impractical for companies to offer better terms (higher signing bonuses or higher starting salaries) to potential high performers; often everyone gets the same mediocre offer, even if some would be better fits than others.

Compare these grossly unscientific traditional hiring processes to the data-driven methods used in the NFL draft. Each year, professional football teams sequentially pick among the top rookie prospects—in general, the worst team in the league gets the first selection, and then teams proceed in order through hundreds of candidates. Drafting a player gives the team only the right to negotiate; it doesn't guarantee that the player will actually agree to a deal. A team that has successfully drafted players must still pay a significant (often more than $1 million) cash bonus to its top draft picks in order to persuade them to sign a contract and play with the team. It's only by carefully measuring and comparing draftees' prior performance, on the basis of vast amounts of data and statistics from their college careers, that NFL teams are able to easily spot the top talent, then lure them with multimillion-dollar signing bonuses. Unlike in most corporate hiring, the top performers are offered substantially larger sums than the mediocre performers. For example, in 2002, the #1 NFL pick, David Carr, received a $10,200,000 cash bonus; the last pick, Ahmad Miller, just $21,000.[5] By offering more up front to those they predict to be higher performers, teams are able to invest wisely in their top talent without overpaying midgrade players.

In the pre-DAMM world, companies couldn't rank candidates for jobs the same ways that NFL teams rank their potential draft picks—a résumé or work history could not yet be broken down in the same way as the NFL teams break college football careers down into yards, tackles, receptions, and other statistics (let alone all the other information gleaned from hours of video footage covering every play). But now the corporate world is catching up to football: in a world where everything we do *can* be digitized, quantified, and analyzed like a football statistic, your professional reputation can mean the difference between whether you are offered a million-dollar signing bonus or a meager starting salary (or not offered the job at all). In the same way that pro football recruiters know the exact dollar value of every tackle, every yard, and every completion—and aren't shy about applying that information in negotiations— every word on your résumé can now be given a dollar value, and every candidate can be stack-ranked. Thus your job search in the future will be more like the NFL draft: a tough set of evaluations followed by personalized negotiations and, for top picks, an offer of substantial value—and less like the old handshakes-and-standard-pay methods of old.

To address the gap between hiring and performance, hiring managers at all kinds of companies are starting to rely on a form of reputation similar to the acqui-hire—by collecting real-world test data that simulates a real job. In Silicon Valley, programmers are being asked to complete a simple programming challenge (not a "brain-teaser," but rather an example that simulates actual on-the-job performance) designed to weed out the pretenders; in the publishing industry, aspiring editorial assistants are asked to demonstrate their ability to edit a manuscript; call-center reps are being asked to show how they would handle a sample call with a (fake) belligerent customer; and more.

In the near future, improved computer reputation screening will provide a way for all companies to rank and evaluate their hires on the basis of data about past performance, just like NFL players. Soon computers will scan the early work done by hundreds (or even thousands) of potential employees and will identify those who will perform one or two standard deviations above the mean. These extremely talented few will be recruited heavily and offered salaries and signing bonuses straight out of college (or even without college at all, as is discussed in chapter 6); the rest will be put on a slower hiring track, without the glamour and lucre.

The coming improvements in digital hiring screening will

have a very tangible effect on the bank accounts of those selected for the top positions. The more accurate hiring screening becomes, the greater the likelihood that the best candidates for every position (not just programmers and engineers) will be able to collect larger salaries and bonuses, because if companies can identify the best candidates early, they can afford to pay more of the programmer's lifetime value up front. As more companies discover the importance of digital hiring methods, there will be increasing competition for the best employees, and firms will have to offer more lucrative packages to standout candidates in order to stay competitive. Thus better "fits" between companies and employees will increase the value to both sides.

In the preceding chapter we read about how companies are using software not only to screen for minimum requirements and automatic disqualifiers but to rank candidates on the basis of their desirability. But this is only the first step in automated hiring; there is potential for computers to do much more than just rank candidates on the basis of simple keyword lists. Thus companies are actively investing in going even further into evaluating potential hires, and for good reason: there's big money to be made in improving employment practices. Employee turnover is costly; some estimate that it costs an average of $10,000 to hire and train a new worker, all of which is lost if the employee is a bad fit and quits or can't perform the job,[6] and the cost is even higher for professional and executive positions. Of course, fast turnover is harmful to employees too: they wind up unemployed again after wasting time interviewing and training for a job that is not a good match. The Employment Policy Foundation estimated that, across all industries, employee turnover created a $713 billion drag on the U.S. economy in 2004 (more than the U.S. federal and state governments spend, combined, on primary education each year).[7]

Given the amount of money at stake, it's no surprise that an entire industry has emerged around what the *New York Times* has called "the human-capital-allocation market," which is basically a fancy term for matching the right applicants with the right jobs. Start-ups like Good.Co, Evolv, and Prophecy Sciences, for example, have come up with increasingly creative ways to digitally screen or "test" potential employees on the various traits the hiring company has deemed to be predictive of job success; one company called Knack even uses video games (like its "Wasabi Waiter" game, in which, as the name suggests, the applicant plays a waiter at a sushi restaurant) to screen for creativity, focus, and interpersonal skills.

It's only a matter of time before computers are able to predict, down to the dollar, how valuable potential candidates will be—on the basis of everything from their productivity, to the odds of their embezzling from the company, to the likelihood of their leaving for another job. Paradoxically, the "best" candidates with the most honors and awards may not rank highly in this type of screening: overqualified candidates may be likely to leave for other jobs sooner if there isn't a good internal promotion pathway. (This tendency to reject the best candidates resembles the "Tufts Syndrome" in university applications, named for Tufts University, located just outside Boston, which became notorious for rejecting overqualified applicants that it thought were more likely to ultimately attend nearby Harvard or MIT.) Police departments are notorious for rejecting applicants with both the lowest and the highest scores on the entrance exam; though lawsuits challenge the practice, police departments have successfully argued that they don't want candidates who are likely to leave for other jobs.[8] Lesson: make sure you know the ideal *range* of scores for any job you're applying for—in many cases being scored too high (whether on a test or by a DAMM algorithm) can be just as toxic as scoring too low.

This next form of computer screening will complete the move from "gut instinct" hiring to a draftlike process that uses extensive digital data to rank employees. Potential employers will look at everything from the career paths of other people who went to your college or university, to your writing style, to any typos in your application. New screening technology will consider every facet of your reputation that is available in digital form— ranging from your online behavior to scores relating to your work performance to the employment status of your Facebook and LinkedIn friends. All of this will be fed into a computer model that will be based on millions of observations of similar people: for a company like Walmart that employs more than 2 million people worldwide, it will be easy to develop a sophisticated regression model of employee quality and retention. In a way, this stage of computerized ranking and screening will be based on the reputations of those who preceded you; if people with similar backgrounds were loyal and performed well, you too will have an opportunity. But if people from your college, or with your major, or with similar career experience were not valued employees, you too will be punished. (To the extent that you can identify stars within the company you want to work for, subtly highlight similarities: Were you part of the same organization or do you have similar interests? Have you followed a similar career trajectory? Did you work with the same team or group at a prior employer?)

To think about the future of DAMM scoring, let's return to Alice and Bob, our hypothetical job candidates from chapter 4. At first, a potential employer doesn't know Alice or Bob and certainly doesn't know which will be a better—that is, more valuable—employee. Instead, all the employer has is data that can be used to draw inferences about which candidate is more likely to be the best. This is true whether the employer is using traditional hiring methods (human review of a résumé and an in-person interview) or new Reputation Economy methods of hiring based on digital reputation information. In the case of traditional methods, the employer uses data collected from the résumé (prior jobs, college attended, etc.) and in an interview (gut feelings about "fit," "culture," and "personality") to try to draw an inference about whether the candidate will be a productive team member. The problem is that with traditional methods these inferences are often wrong.

But in the Reputation Economy, employers will have infinitely more data to consider. And, as discussed in chapter 3, increased computer power will allow the data to be analyzed far more quickly and inexpensively. Instead of just looking at Alice's and Bob's résumés, an employer will run a comprehensive computerized analysis of their careers to date. Just as NFL teams look beyond traditional "résumé" information (the college a draft pick attended, or the number of games he won) to rank draft picks with millions of dollars on the line, computerized ranking will allow employers to collect, analyze, and score hundreds of data points about candidates.

When NFL teams draft players, they build computer models to make sense of hundreds (or even thousands) of data points collected in detail over the course of a college career: average yards per rush against good defenses, average fumble rate in rainy weather, number of tackles made (or broken) in the open field. And with ever more sophisticated models, teams can even rank players according to a particular situation or style of play: a player who tends to fumble in the rain may be ill suited for Seattle's winter weather and open-roof stadium, but his weaknesses may be minimized in New Orleans's domed stadium;

similarly, teams that rely on up-the-middle runs may be look-ing for offensive linemen who are predicted to create run open-ings versus linemen who are predicted to hold long pass blocks.[9] Thus teams can predict not only how well a player is likely to play generally but also how well he is likely to perform on that particular team. Imagine if NFL teams were limited to trying to run a draft based only on the equivalent of traditional résumé data: college attended, an in-person "talking" interview, and maybe the total number of wins for that college team (roughly equivalent to a GPA).

When corporate hiring catches up to sports, computers will review every aspect of candidates' digital lives to try to deter-mine if they will be a good fit. This ranges from reviewing the strength of a candidate's network on professional network-ing sites like LinkedIn, to looking for "bad influence" friends on Facebook (even if you are clean and sober, you can be dragged down by drunk, foul-mouthed, bankruptcy-declaring, company-badmouthing friends), to assessing the tenor of any newspaper or blog mentions of the candidate (positive? neg-ative? indifferent?), to credit score data (when this is legal to obtain). After all, as was discussed in chapter 4, all public data about a candidate will soon be sorted and aggregated into a tidy little score, and these scores will be made publicly available to all.

For jobs where individual contributions can be measured, these screening methods will aggregate every measure of past performance as well. Companies in some industries—like tech—are almost already there. For example, returning to the programmers Alice and Bob, one of the oldest measures of the quantity of output of programmers is the number of lines of code they produce per unit of time. One "KLOC" is one thousand (K) lines of code (LOC). KLOC is hardly a complete measurement—it's possible for an efficient programmer to produce fewer high-quality lines of code and for an inefficient programmer to produce a large volume of bug-ridden code—which is why advanced screening methods will also look at measures of quality. When a programmer is able to provide a code sample (whether it's a publicly available project on a site like GitHub, discussed in chapter 9, or an internal piece of code shown confidentially), that code can be analyzed for quality on the basis of factors such as compilation errors or whether it passes so-called unit tests to assess functionality.

In addition to simply providing more information about a candidate's individual performance and traits, DAMM techniques will allow employers to identify an individual's contributions to teams. In the world of knowledge work, flat organizations, and project-based management (to name just a few popular business buzzwords), one of the most important skills of an employee is the ability to effectively work on teams and contribute to joint projects. But current hiring methods struggle to identify the value of individual contributors to projects; a traditional résumé may list the accomplishments of your team, but it doesn't really have a way of isolating your individual contributions to that team. (Incidentally, this is yet another reason for the acqui-hire trend, where the whole team is taken as a unit, maximizing the chance that the purchaser will end up with the most valuable team members, even if it's not possible to identify those MVPs in advance.)

One common bias of current hiring methods is known as "failed-project syndrome" and several similar terms. In short, candidates who were part of a large project that failed are often tarnished by the project's failure, even if their performance had nothing to do with the project's failure. They may have been the most valuable contributors and done everything possible to pull the project back from the brink but been stopped by forces outside their control. Conversely, mediocre candidates who were at the right place at the right time get ahead by attaching their names to a successful project even if the project succeeded *despite* their efforts.

Put another way, the problem is that the current system often fails to distinguish "good candidates on bad teams" from "bad candidates on good teams." This is a problem familiar to sports teams faced with recruiting choices. In many sports, success depends on players working together, and many good players make contributions that don't show up in the score sheets: good passes, effective defense, and so on. Often, a good player is burdened by a poor team, or a bad player has managed to collect apparent successes by playing for a good team. To counteract this influence, sports teams have created scores like the "+/− score" (or "plus-minus score"). As one simple example, the +/− score for hockey is calculated by just adding up the number of goals scored by the team when a player is on the ice and subtracting the number of goals scored by the opposition during the same time. So, for example, if Alice's hockey team scored three goals while she was playing and had two goals scored against it while she was playing, Alice would have a score of +1. By ranking players on a team by their +/− score, it is possible to identify which players are most likely to be contributing positively to the team's performance, even if they aren't scoring goals directly.

Thanks to advances in data analysis, it is now possible to construct a similar +/− score for job candidates and other individuals who will work on many team projects over the course of their careers. Comparing the performance of teams with the candidate to teams *without* the candidate over the course of enough projects makes it possible to isolate the contributions (or lack thereof) made by one individual. To return to our example of computer programmers, it is often possible to measure whether a team's project was successfully launched, on time and without bugs. Each individual's contributions to that project are aggregated with the contributions of others, making it difficult to directly evaluate any individual. But by adding up the successes (or failures) of a particular employee as she works with different teams one can get a sense of whether the individual is contributing positively to the teams she joins. Other teamwork-intensive jobs can be ranked similarly: attorneys, surgeons, managers, writers, editors, and nearly anyone else who works on a team whose success or failure can be measured and aggregated by a computer. Each of these jobs features discrete projects where different people contribute to teams at different times, allowing a computer to tease out the value of individual contributors by comparing teams with and without that person. The desired outcome, of course, may vary—a healthy patient, a *New York Times* bestseller, or a win for a client in court—but the method of teasing out individual performance holds constant across these fields.

In the Reputation Economy, not only will scoring software isolate an individual candidate's contributions from those of his or her teammates, but the software will consider the reputation of the team or company itself. For example, imagine that Alice spent three years working for Zynga, the briefly high-flying social game production studio. However, when Alice starts looking for a new job, Zynga is suffering from a crisis in its own reputation; social games are being panned, and Zynga's stock is down more than 80 percent from its IPO peak. In a traditional hiring world, interviewers would associate Alice with Zynga's failed games (whether consciously or subconsciously), even though in all likelihood Alice's individual contributions had nothing to do with the company's 80 percent stock crash. In the Reputation Economy, computer algorithms would be able to correlate Alice's contributions at the company to the swings in its performance and profitability.

If Andy Warhol were a young artist today, his life would have been very different: digital has changed everything. Forget Warhol's being picked for the 1964 show solely on the basis of word of mouth. Today, search engines rank search results for "best upcoming artists," sites like Flickr automatically rank photos and art on the basis of how "interesting" users find them, and art discussion sites automatically generate lists of the "hottest" artists based on how many people are discussing the topics.

Today, graphic designers are doing much the same as Warhol: grinding out portfolio pieces looking for opportunity. But now they can do it digitally rather than by crisscrossing the country, soup cans in hand. For example, the graphic design chat site DeviantART allows designers to post, discuss, and rate each other's artwork. It is not just limited to new graduates either; in just one of many examples, professional illustrator Lauren Faust, who is best known for rebooting the *My Little Pony* franchise with its *Friendship Is Magic* incarnation, and who was an active user of the site for years before getting the *My Little Pony* job, built her artistic credibility within the relatively small network of professional designers and illustrators, then later built buzz for the series reboot by posting early artwork to the site.

Similarly, freelance design sites like 99designs have allowed promising young designers to get a foot in the door in the design world by showcasing their portfolios online. The 99designs site has launched more than 150,000 paid design gigs, many of which have led to full-time paid jobs.

The key to each of these design-related sites is that they all allow the creation of easily rankable portfolios that can grow stronger over time. On each site, portfolios are rated, voted, and judged, building a record that can easily be measured: Carl's portfolio scored 70 points, Denise's scored 90, and so on. It's easy for a potential employer to rank the tens of thousands of designers on any site to identify the select few that might be good enough for a particular job.

This is exactly why programmers have become more proactive about showing off their credentials. Instead of setting up entire businesses as their portfolio, they are publicizing "reputation scores" they have earned on sites like Stack Overflow and Coderwall. Users earn points on the former by answering programming questions posted by the public and on the latter by participating in other coding sites and uploading brief snippets of advice. Both sites claim to offer replacements for (or at least supplements to) traditional résumés, and companies are using both to rank and identify talented programmers without the trouble (and additional expense) of an acqui-hire.

As the Reputation Economy matures, these kinds of sites will become more and more common, even in industries that, unlike coding and graphic design, don't produce tangible products. Indeed, thanks to the ever-increasing sophistication of computer scoring, soon virtually all professionals will be similarly ranked alongside each other. Here are some tips for how to rise to the top, no matter what your chosen field may be.

How to Become a Celebrity Hire

In the world of Reputation Economy hiring techniques, some individuals have already figured out how to optimize their chance of being identified as a key contributor—and in turn earn top salaries, signing bonuses, and other rewards. For example, the founders of sites like Drop.io who have figured out how to hack the hiring process by creating an acqui-hire have shown that they understand how to cultivate the kind of reputation that demonstrates value. But how?

For one, by building a portfolio project (in the form of a start-up business in the case of acqui-hires) they gave potential employers *something tangible* that other candidates couldn't match. Tangible portfolios could run the gamut from a business case study (for a manager or a consultant) to an award or a certificate (for a lawyer, a teacher, a doctor, or some other professional) to a literal portfolio (for a designer or an artist).

Take the example of author and speaker Gary Vaynerchuk (often simply "Gary Vee"). Born in the USSR, he moved to the United States when young and eventually began working in his father's liquor store in Springfield Township, New Jersey. Vaynerchuk knew that he was outgoing and entertaining— and he wanted to do more than work at a small wineshop—but he had no way to prove his credentials for any other job. So he started with what he knew: he started a podcast about wine (*Wine Library TV*) in which he enthusiastically reviewed literally thousands of wines. The content was solid and was presented in a unique way: if wine appreciation had traditionally been done in hushed tones and golf claps, Vaynerchuk brought a *Mad Money* approach with over-the-top enthusiasm for wines he loved. The show grew a dedicated following among wine lovers—and among people who never knew they would like a wine show. On the basis of his fast-growing audience, Vaynerchuk was to interview guests ranging from Wayne Gretzky to Dick Vermeil to Jim Cramer himself. Having proved his ability to capture an audience, Vaynerchuk began to pursue his real passion: marketing and business. He signed a ten-book deal with an advance of $1 million and began to publish books like *Crush It!* and *The Thank You Economy,* describing his philosophy on work, business, and the new economy. And it all started from a simple podcast describing wines available at his father's shop that became an effective portfolio piece for his book deal and subsequent successes.

Of course, these portfolios should prove your *ability to perform at the specific task for which you are being hired.* Remember that, for an employer, the hiring process is all about uncertainty. Many new hires just don't work out, and turnover costs the hiring firm time, money, and management attention. By creating a portfolio project that mimics the work you will be doing day in and day out, you increase your value to employers by taking some of the uncertainty out of the hiring process. In other words, the founders of acqui-hired companies proved that they could do the work, day in and day out; and Gary Vee proved that he was capable of creating an audience for nearly any kind of content. Similarly, for other types of jobs and industries, you want to build a reputation for the exact skills for which you want to be hired.

At the same time, though, it's also good to show off your nontraditional credentials. By showing off nontraditional credentials, people rich with reputation have demonstrated how they are uniquely qualified for the positions they seek. In some cases, there is no credential that fits their perfect job. (What college degree tells you that somebody will be a social media expert? Gary Vee figured that he'd make his own credential for it.) In others, it takes proving that your new credential is better than the old. And since most of the jobs with the most value to you may never even be posted, you have no way of knowing what quirky or seemingly unrelated skills the employer (and its algorithms) might view as a selling point. So be sure all your nontraditional skills—maybe you are certified in scuba diving, have won awards for your poetry, or know how to hot-wire a car—are mentioned somewhere. Will they trigger the computer to choose you for that high-paying job from among the thousands of qualified candidates (with the same traditional skills) like you? No way of knowing. But they *will* help you stand out.

Last, these successful candidates *worked outside the normal job negotiation process.* For most candidates, working inside the typical hiring process, maximum salary and bonus are set within a range provided to the human resources department by faceless "management" tasked with budgeting for hires up to a year in advance. This everyday hiring system has very limited flexibility to recognize extraordinary talent: management sets the budget and HR follows it, no matter how good a candidate may seem. But by building the kind of reputation that draws recruiters and employers to *you,* you can often bypass the human resources department and negotiate with your individual department, or even your individual manager, who usually has the leeway to spend at a higher level than might be dictated by some preestablished HR chart.

No matter what profession or industry you're in, a good reputation can open doors you never knew existed. But your career is far from the only area in your life where you stand to profit from a good reputation. In the coming chapters we'll talk about all the ways you can leverage your digital reputation for greater opportunities, perks, and social benefits in myriad other areas.

6

Disruptive

Reeducating Education

T HESE DAYS, COLLEGE IS MORE POPULAR THAN EVER. A near-record 70 percent of U.S. high school graduates continue to college, up from 60 percent in 1990 and 50 percent in 1980.[1] Enrollment is booming worldwide as well. For example, Yale recently opened a campus in Singapore, forming that nation's first liberal arts college. NYU is opening campuses everywhere from Buenos Aires to Sydney to Abu Dhabi. Mainland China is also experiencing an unprecedented boom in higher education: depending on the data source and definition of *college* used, the number of college students in China increased from around 12 million in 2001 to around 20 million in 2005, and some estimates put it over 25 million as of 2007 (the difficulty in even estimating the number of students is a symptom of the rapid growth of the Chinese college market).[2] Of course, any of these estimates dwarfs the U.S. figures of around 9 million students enrolled in U.S. full-time four-year programs and 3 million in U.S. full-time two-year programs in 2011.[3]

At the same time, tuition and spending are at all-time highs. Students are paying huge sums of money—up to $200,000 in tuition alone for four years of private college and often over $50,000 for public colleges (not to mention the opportunity cost of spending four years in school rather than working or exploring other pursuits) and racking up massive debts—for the dubious distinction of an undergraduate degree. And the situation is only getting worse: tuition has been increasing at a rate of 8 percent per year,[4] almost double the rate of inflation for other goods and services, and higher than almost any other category other than health care. In the United States alone, more than $425 billion is spent annually on traditional college education (not even including for-profit schools),[5] and this cost doesn't include the massive personal spending by college students themselves (on everything from textbooks to togas).

But despite the growth of college enrollment and spending, employers are still complaining that they aren't getting job applicants with the skills they need. Some studies suggest that almost half of college students make no gains in written communication or critical thinking in their first two years of college,[6] and even the former president of Harvard, who spent more than twenty years in the role, laments that "colleges and universities, for all the benefits they bring, accomplish far less for their students than they should" and that "many seniors graduate without being able to write well enough to satisfy their employers."[7] Yet employers still rely on college degrees as a way to quickly filter applicants, despite the fear that they are getting students without actual education.

On the flip side of the astronomical sums American students

pay to attend college are the immense resources that the higher education system spends educating students. Colleges spend billions annually on professors, teaching assistants, audiovisual equipment, lab equipment, test-taking software, Scantron readers, and more. To give just three examples, Stanford spends $4.4 billion per year,[8] the University of Texas spends $2.2 billion annually,[9] and the Ohio State University spends more than $5 billion per year.[10] Each of these three colleges spent more in 2012 than the entire GDP of Belize (around $1.4 billion), and the total annual spending by colleges in the United States of around $425 billion exceeds the GDP of major countries, including Austria, Thailand, and Venezuela.

States too are spending billions subsidizing postsecondary education. So students are burdened by increasing debt, and state budget makers, already squeezed, are finding it hard to justify spending on state universities, thus putting what *used to be* a relatively affordable state-subsidized education even more beyond the reach of most students.

At the same time there is increasing evidence that this one-size-fits-all traditional four-year model of on-campus education is a poor fit for many students. For starters, some students can advance more quickly, while others take longer to achieve the same goals. Some students have outside responsibilities—a family or an eldercare situation—that requires time away from the classroom or restricts them geographically. Some students need extra time to mature before starting college; others are emotionally and intellectually ready earlier than the traditional entrance age of eighteen or nineteen. Others have learning styles simply not suited for classroom learning; plenty of extremely intelligent (and potentially successful people) are simply "wired" for project-oriented work or teamwork rather than lectures and exams, and many otherwise excellent students struggle with the conformity required to succeed in a rigid academic system. And *all* students would be better served by less student loan debt. To top it off, in addition to unhappiness among students and taxpayers, there is increasing concern about competitiveness of U.S. college graduates relative to their peers in Europe and Asia.

Beyond the exorbitant cost, and the tension with students' individual goals and life circumstances, there are many other problems inherent in the traditional model of higher education. Yet colleges have tolerated those problems because nobody has managed to invent a better system that meets all of the criteria required of a higher education system, including the ability to work at a scale of millions of students per year.

One problem with the one-size-fits-all system is reflected in the varying size of institutions: small colleges don't have the resources for specialization, but large colleges suffer from bureaucratic rigidity. For example, a small school may have only one professor to cover all of East Asian history, despite there being at least six major traditions that are more different than they are alike. By contrast, large colleges have the resources for more specialized instruction (at a major research university, there may be an expert in ancient China and another in modern China, and there may even be a professor specializing in just the Qing dynasty), but they need extremely standardized administrative processes to keep everything running smoothly. Managing a campus of tens of thousands of students—small cities in their own right—requires standardized scheduling and registration in order to prevent hundreds of students from showing up for one class while tens of other classes go empty. Universities like Texas A&M and University of Texas–Austin, which each enroll more than fifty thousand students on their main campuses (they say everything is bigger in Texas), have to have extremely complex course enrollment procedures in order to handle so many students at once; as just one example, A&M has more than ten different course registration deadlines for each semester, depending on class year, honors status, employment, and other factors. Graduating requires as much skill in navigating the system as it requires actual learning, and many students end up graduating without taking their desired courses (or sometimes even their preferred major)—let alone getting the skills they need to succeed in the real world.

But despite these plentiful concerns about the "fit" of college for many individuals, students still line up for college because the credential of having a college degree (especially from a "good school") is necessary to even get past the résumé-screening stage for many jobs. As a result many students are forced into the expensive, time-consuming traditional model that just doesn't fit their learning style, family circumstances, or career goals. The lengths students go to in order to get their credential persist despite the fact that a college degree is a notoriously ineffective signal; it's just heavily used because, as we'll discuss throughout this chapter, it's better than any common alternative that employers use.

No More Pencils, No More Books

In the West, college currently serves at least two major functions with respect to the job market. Let's call these two functions "education" and "signaling." By *education*, we mean the function of actually imparting skills and knowledge to students, ranging from general critical thinking to specific technical knowledge. The amount of knowledge that students retain from their lectures and exams is hotly questioned, but, especially in technical fields, employers hope that students learn *something* from their bright college years.

By *signaling,* we mean the ability of a college degree to inform employers that a given student is likely to be capable of performing at a high level. Most employers believe that, in the absence of any other information, it's a good bet that an applicant with a college degree is more likely to succeed in almost any job than somebody without a college degree. They may also believe that an applicant with a degree from a prestigious university is more likely to succeed in a job than an applicant from a college with a reputation for mediocrity. Of course, nobody thinks that simply holding a degree is a *guarantee* that an applicant will succeed; instead, when one is faced with hundreds (or even thousands) of résumés, the presence or absence of a degree is simply a quick way to filter and deal with the overload of applications.

A perfect example of the key difference between educating and signaling comes from an unlikely place: the Department of Motor Vehicles. In many states, the process of learning to drive (education) occurs through a public or private driver's ed course that is largely separated from the dreaded behind-the-wheel test administered by a battle-hardened tester at the local DMV that credentials you as a licensed driver (signaling). In other words, the organization that gives a driving credential (the DMV) is different from the organization that does the actual educating (driver's ed). The decoupled system works: people can choose from hundreds of driver's ed providers, but at the end of the day everyone has to pass the same rigorous driving exam. This is not the case in the current college environment, where the people doing both the teaching *and* the signaling (college and professors) are incentivized to make students look better, thus undermining the value of both the signaling *and* the educating (through grade inflation, diploma mills, etc.).

In the coming years, the unraveling of these tensions will

cause significant changes in higher education. In this chapter we'll talk about how the Reputation Economy will hasten that change by destabilizing traditional education methods—and sometimes decoupling the functions of educating and signaling in powerful ways. A new system will emerge, leaner, more efficient, and more powerful than ever. The winners will be those who are ready to adapt to the new rules and who take advantage of new opportunities to prove their unique value to the world. This chapter will show you how to be one of them.

The traditional model of higher education continues because, until recently, there has not been a viable alternative credentialing system. One widely touted alternative to the traditional system is online learning. After all, today, an increasing fraction of world knowledge is available online, and in increasingly structured forms. Some parts of college can't be replicated online exactly (many social interactions in college and bench research), but many can (lectures, papers, exams, etc.), and some can be done even more richly online than in traditional college (interactive problem sets that adjust difficulty based on success, data-driven analysis of strengths and weaknesses, etc.). Online customized education could also solve many of the logistical problems of large colleges: students could plan their own schedules at their own pace, eliminating class conflicts and long hikes across campus. Students could also pick the best lectures from the best professors anywhere in the world (at least in theory) and receive seminar-like support from smaller groups. But until recently students' online options have been limited to a handful of for-profit online colleges and a few traditional universities trying to port their lecture-style classes online. Each has been largely a digital replica of traditional education: classes around an hour long, scheduled on the basis of a semester, and often requiring live interactions at fixed times. This problem of carrying over the worst features of an old model when a new system is invented is hardly new: consider how early cars were so similar to horse-drawn carriages that the driver of early cars needlessly sat outside in the rain while the passengers rode inside. Early online education is much the same; it is too literal a copy of the offline model. The result is an online experience that fails to solve many of the difficulties of traditional education.

Until recently, it was difficult to have a meaningful online learning experience. At best, a student could watch YouTube videos and read online discussions—and even if there was plenty of material to work with, there was the issue of credibility. Pick your favorite subject—economics, environmental studies, religion, race relations—and it's all but certain to be rife with cranks, so even for the most discerning and critical self-learners any attempt at undirected self-education on those topics will involve wasting time disentangling fiction from fact, simply because the loudest voice online is not necessarily the most correct. Part of the value of traditional education is forced credentialing of those doing the teaching; you might not agree with your professor's point of view, but the system is set up to encourage dissenting views among academics and the ability to accurately identify the state of the debate.

But even if a student managed to overcome all these obstacles and somehow obtain a top-notch online education, it wouldn't matter for the second reason why college is important: signaling. Prior to the Reputation Economy, the credentialing value of self-directed online learning was not much better than that of no education at all. Most employers won't take "I taught myself American history by watching a bunch of history videos on YouTube" as the equivalent of a degree—yet. That's because the second crucial function of college—and the function that has allowed college to exist in its current form despite all of its inefficiencies—is to send a signal that, on average, a college graduate is likely to be more employable than a high school graduate. The Reputation Economy is poised to replace all those traditional signals with new signals that can communicate *actual learning* more clearly and at lower cost for everybody.

More Than Just a Sheepskin?

There's no question that signaling is a huge part of the value of a college education. Employers are more likely to hire students with degrees than without, almost universally. They are also more likely to hire (and pay a premium for) students with "brand-name" diplomas from leading four-year colleges than graduates of other programs. Ironically, this is true regardless of the college performance of any particular individual: the bottom student at Harvard is (fairly or unfairly) more likely to be picked for many jobs than the top student at many other schools. (What do you call the last-place graduate of medical school? "Doctor.") Employers take "college degree" as such a strong signal that students without a college degree (even if they also have a high-quality nontraditional educational background) simply never have the opportunity to prove themselves, because, as we've discussed, their résumés get automatically filtered out by computers in the first stages of hiring, while college graduates advance onward to interviews and other evaluations.

And while it's true that Ivy League and other elite schools spend more on education per student than other schools, this difference in education spending alone doesn't explain the difference in salaries for graduates of, for example, Harvard, Hanover, and New Hampshire State. This powerful effect of a degree even has a fancy name in academic circles: the "sheepskin effect," named after the old term for college diplomas, which actually were delivered on sheep hides until high-quality paper became more affordable. (At the University of Notre Dame, undergraduate diplomas were delivered on real sheepskins until the class of 2012, and one religious high school in Virginia still annually delivers its diplomas on the real thing.)

In formal economics literature, the sheepskin effect measures the difference in job and salary prospects between candidates with education histories that are equal except for the fact that one received a degree and the other did not. The difference, as it turns out, is stark. For example, a 2008 Canadian review of prior studies noted that if two candidates went to four years of college but one received a diploma and the other did not (even for reasons outside her control, such as courses being unavailable or degree requirements changing), the one without the degree would receive only 70 percent of the increase in salary one would normally expect from a college degree. Even after controlling for any differences between the groups (noting that college dropouts may have lower grades on average or be different in other ways), the authors of the study were still able to identify substantial differences in earnings potential between the holders of degrees and otherwise identical candidates without degrees. As they put it, "Sheepskin effects remain large even when directly observed skill measures are included in the earnings equation," and they surmised that the remaining effect was largely due to the signaling effect of college.[11] Another study found that, holding all else constant, completing a degree gave more than an 11 percent boost to the salary of a student in his twenties compared to that of somebody with the same years of education.[12]

In more informal conversation, the sheepskin effect is simply the fact that it's often easier for someone with a degree to get a job, even if another candidate has more experience or better skills. Put simply, employers—be they businesses, nonprofits, universities, government agencies, you name it—are busy and need a way to quickly sort candidates; how else do you measure a candidate's aptitude for jobs in the increasingly complex knowledge economy that require blending teamwork with skills from a variety of domains? Some employers have tried, at great expense: the City of New Haven tried to use a written exam to identify promising candidates for promotion within the city's fire department, but just developing the test required interviews and ride-alongs with its own personnel, interviews of fire departments in other cities, and testing of exam versions on its own current personnel. And, in the end, the test led to a legal fight that went all the way to the Supreme Court. Even if the test had been the most accurate way to predict performance in an emergency situation (which is itself an open question), it was an incredibly time-consuming and expensive venture for the city, and certainly not one likely to be adopted by many employers or companies.

Traditional interviewing provides no better signal: candidates who interview well don't always perform well. In fact, many psychologists and management scientists have found that there's only a weak correlation between performance in job interviews and performance on the job. Each study has found slightly different results depending on who happens to be interviewing and how later job performance is measured, but most report that unstructured job interviews (traditional "tell me about yourself" and "what are your goals" interviews) have a validity of around 0.35, or 35 percent.[13] A validity score of 0 would mean that interviews have no relationship at all to job performance; flipping a coin would be no better way to select among candidates. By contrast, a score of 1 is the holy grail of performance evaluation: it would mean that interviews would be able to perfectly predict performance. So a score of .35 is better than nothing at all, but it lags vastly behind other methods. By contrast, the combination of a general aptitude test with a work sample test (actually performing the job at hand) is among the best methods yet discovered and can generate a test validity of up to .63. However, a general aptitude test is often illegal, and a work sample test can be expensive and difficult to administer. Imagine what it would take to make a complete work sample for a firefighter: everything from CPR to entering burning buildings to search-and-rescue. Such an evaluation would be complete, but it would cost thousands of dollars per candidate—at that price, departments would have to narrow the field of candidates before administering the test, bringing everything back full circle to college and grades.

Interviewing is also subject to bias; it is so bad that one study found that interviewers focused primarily on nonverbal cues sent by the candidate (such as the candidate's clothing and self-confidence) instead of actual job qualifications. One MIT study was even able to predict the results of 85 percent of simulated job interviews only on the basis of the speaking styles of the interviewer and candidate, without even considering the substance of the interview.[14]

So for lack of a better way to screen candidates that is both fast (Can you tell by looking at a résumé?) and affordable (Does it require any special equipment or testing?), employers turn to the known standard as the first step: they look for a college degree and a GPA. Of course, many employers who just ask for a college degree aren't actually looking at the things a candidate learned in college. Anything that a candidate learned (and remembers!) from History 205: China 202 B.C.–A.D. 1271 is not nearly as useful to an employer as the *signal* that the candidate is motivated, able to learn, willing to work hard in order to achieve a goal, and so on. Some employers are looking for students who studied more specific skill sets in college—teaching, engineering, dental technology—but often find that even these students still graduate college with a very low level of *practical* skills and still often require extensive on-the-job training. To the extent that a college degree is a signal, it's a relatively weak one.

This would matter much less if colleges made it easy to rank students from different schools comparatively. Instead, it's notoriously difficult to compare students: GPAs differ wildly across colleges, majors, and specialties, often more on the basis of the political power of the department than on any difference in student quality. Not only has the dramatic increase in grade inflation (the fact that college grades are, on average, much higher than a generation ago—so much so that the median [middle] student at an average private college will have a GPA of around 3.3, an increase of 0.2 in the last twenty years and an increase of almost 0.8 since the 1960s) made it difficult to identify high-performing students within schools, it has also made comparisons across schools much more difficult because some schools have held the line on grade inflation more than others. For example, New Hampshire's small liberal arts college Saint Anselm has fixed its median GPA at 2.5, a full 0.8 (almost a whole letter grade) below that of its peers. In other words, a 3.0 GPA is a lot harder to come by at Saint Anselm than your average private college—it's the difference between being in the top and bottom halves of the class. Some schools, such as Brown University, even seem to take pride in making it difficult to compare grades and ranks among students: there, students can take all, none, or any number of their classes on a pass/ fail basis, or they can request a narrative explanation of their performance in any class in lieu of grades. The result is a mix of students with conventional graded transcripts, students with many pass/fail selections, and students with written evaluations from select professors combined with any of the above—and in each case it's not knowable to what extent students gamed the system by requesting letter grades in easy courses or from easy graders.

While this system encourages the consideration of each student as a unique snowflake, it makes the initial screening process difficult for employers: employers just want to know if a student is likely to perform better or worse than a peer at another school, and narrative evaluations (each written by a different professor with different quirks and standards) are difficult to compare with each other and to conventional transcripts. With employers facing hundreds of applications (nationally, around 250 résumés are sent for every job posting made), this system just doesn't scale.[15]

But even at schools where grades are mandatory, students are graded on a strict curve, and ranks are published, there's not much information for employers to go on. At the end of the day, there's a simple dilemma in grading: the stricter the grading policy, the more likely that top students achieved their rank by choosing classes exclusively on the basis of their strengths (think of the bilingual Spanish-English student enrolling in a Spanish class, or the editor of his high school newspaper enrolling in Journalism 101) instead of learning new material; the looser the grading policy, the more likely that top students achieved their rank by taking advantage of the grading policy (think of the student taking the notorious premed class in organic chemistry pass/fail but taking Music Studies 101—at many schools derided as "clapping for credit"—for a letter grade).

And of course, good grades in one area completely divorced from a job description are all but useless; the straight-A philosophy major who spends all day thinking critically about the social contract might be a great Ph.D. candidate but a lousy computer programmer. One engineering major might make a great fit at Google but fare poorly at NASA; a different engineering major with the same transcript might do exactly the opposite.

Despite all these flaws, employers have no choice but to fall back on the age-old combination of college, major, and GPA to do much of their hiring screening. One recent study showed that almost 80 percent of employers used a strict GPA cutoff for candidates.[16] Just look at these recent job advertisements: a company in Newport Beach requires that candidates "have completed a B.A. or B.S. degree with a reasonable GPA" to even apply for its research associate position,[17] and the U.S. Central Intelligence Agency says, "New college graduates we hire for positions within the CIA must have at least a 3.0 GPA on a 4.0 scale," without any adjustment for grade inflation across different schools.

If a new signal of employability is to displace the university degree, it will have to do better at balancing the cost to employers (low) and accuracy (also low) of a university diploma in predicting job performance. And as we've discussed in earlier chapters, there's money in getting hiring filtering right: for every percentage point better that a new screening mechanism performs over the old method of just looking for a diploma, employers will realize significant value, from the value of an hour of the HR manager's time to the cost of plane tickets across the country, a hotel, and a full day of staff time spent interviewing, to the turnover cost of a bad hire and subsequent termination.

Thanks to the Reputation Economy, the signals used by employers are changing again. In the future the tools of the Reputation Economy will empower both applicants and employers to predict how well a candidate's actual skills—not his GPA or the name of the institution that granted his diploma—are suited for the particular position or company. In other words, the Reputation Economy will be so disruptive to higher education because the technology is quickly developing to allow *your* unique reputation to become a stronger signal of employability than the name on your diploma, or even whether you have a diploma at all. And, most importantly, thanks to the new technology being developed in the DAMM world, these signals will be increasingly easy and cost effective for employers.

College: Time to Split the Baby

Perhaps not surprisingly, the real disruptors in education will come from outside the academy. Indeed, the most important changes to education in the next twenty years won't be of the sort made by bureaucrats deciding whether to have twenty-four or twenty-six students in a classroom, or whether students should take four or five classes in a given field, or whether laptops or tablets are the best tools for e-learning. Instead, reform will lead to a true break from the current tradition of four-year colleges with lectures, dorms, and final exams that all lead to a fancy diploma and a single canonical GPA. Yet despite all the hype about online learning, MOOCs (massive open online courses), and the like, the most powerful change won't be in the way that education is actually delivered: in the end, it won't matter whether students learn online, in the classroom, through an apprenticeship, or by some method that hasn't even been invented yet. The most important change will be to the way that students and job applicants are *measured*. And that change in measurement will turn the current signaling system on its head.

An unlikely education reformer named Sal Khan is using

the Reputation Economy to do just that. He is not the person you might expect to be challenging the traditional model of education: he isn't a state governor tired of expensive education budgets, a dean of a major university seeking change from the inside, a politically connected CEO of a for-profit school, or even a professor. He doesn't hold any degrees in education and has never been a full-time teacher. He isn't part of the teachers' union, and he is often criticized by it. Instead, he's a humble math geek with a total of four degrees from Harvard and MIT who embarked on a quest to reform higher education quite accidentally when his nephew happened to ask for math tutoring in 2004. With bachelor's degrees in math and electrical engineering and master's degrees in electrical engineering and computer science, Khan is perhaps as overqualified to teach grade school math as Beethoven would be to give children piano lessons. But when Khan started using Yahoo! Doodle—a chat feature that allows simultaneous audio chat with a shared electronic notepad—to give personal lessons to his nephew, he found the lessons so effective that by 2006 he decided to start posting the videos on YouTube. As the news of unusually effective math tutorials spread, Khan found his audience growing and increased his pace of video uploads to match.

Once he realized he was on to something, he quit a comfortable six-figure job[18] as a hedge fund analyst (what Tom Wolfe would call a "Master of the Universe")[19] to start his own education nonprofit with an unusual and ambitious mission: make the prestigious schools that he attended obsolete, and replace the value of a Harvard diploma with an actual education anyone can achieve—or, as he puts it, "a free world-class education for anyone anywhere."[20]

By 2013, Khan had personally created more than three thousand videos, and the academy's YouTube channel reached more than four hundred thousand subscribers. By 2013, Khan Academy videos had been viewed more than 200 million times. Remarking on how Khan had used little more than a YouTube account and a microphone to launch a movement, Bill Gates said, "This guy is amazing. It is awesome how much he has done with very little in the way of resources."[21]

Today, Khan Academy is perhaps the largest nonprofit online school many people have never heard of. Unlike the for-profit online University of Phoenix, the Khan Academy doesn't advertise on late-night TV or have a professional football stadium named after it (where, ironically, the University of Phoenix has never played a single game because it doesn't have an intercollegiate sports program). Most Khan Academy videos have a quirky style unique to Khan: unlike most video lectures produced by commercial education companies, they are not shot to simulate a traditional classroom. Unlike the traditional videos that show a professor in front of a (real) blackboard and a (usually fake) classroom, Khan's tutorial videos never show his own face. Instead the screen simply shows a steady feed of Khan's digital whiteboard, on which he scrawls notes (in rather poor handwriting) while narrating in a baritone voice-over.

Khan quickly expanded from math tutorials to a more comprehensive vision. The Academy now includes videos on everything from biology to economics to art to cognitive science to capital markets. But Khan's long-term plan goes beyond a comprehensive library of videos. Instead, Khan wants to completely reinvent the higher education experience.[22] In his vision, schools like Harvard and MIT would be replaced with a mix of hands-on internships and self-directed online learning. Diplomas written in Latin and printed on sheepskin would be replaced with credentials earned through online college exams administered nationwide—possibly by the Khan Academy and possibly by other credentialing services. In Khan's vision, it doesn't matter where or how you get the relevant knowledge, so long as you have it—by contrast, good luck showing up at Yale and asking for a diploma because you studied the same subjects at Princeton. In this model, one thousand professors at different schools across the country, each teaching the same introductory computer science class to fifty students each, would be replaced with one professor (hopefully the best, and certainly the best prepared) teaching to a worldwide online audience of fifty thousand students. And perhaps most importantly, these fifty thousand students would receive the exact same credential for having taken it.

As Khan's vision expanded from simple tutoring to a new model of education, he built an infrastructure around the learning experience. Students can register (free), track their lessons (free), use practice math problem sets and interactive games (free), and chat with other students (free). "Coaches" (anyone who is helping a student learn) can also register and track their students' progress. While the online component is still in its infancy, the Khan Academy's model differs in almost every way from traditional full-time education. There is no mandatory curriculum or semester; students can advance as quickly or slowly as they like. Instead of hourlong lectures, content is delivered in bite-sized mini-units, usually in the range of fifteen minutes each. For example, calculus—a course that might be taught in forty-five college lectures—is broken into 192 minilectures of about fifteen minutes each (because there's no class schedule, there's no need for all the lectures to be the exact same length). There are no grades, classrooms, or professors. And, of course, there are no collegiate Gothic buildings with ivy-covered walls, no football stadiums, and no statues— the Khan Academy has done away with all of the trappings of higher education in America. What's left is a nonprofit focused exclusively on the education part of higher education.

Distance learning has been done before. Even correspondence schools existed long before the U.S. Postal Service had even been founded to deliver correspondence: a 1728 advertisement in the *Boston Gazette* touted the services of one Caleb Phillips, who could teach "the new method of Short Hand" by correspondence.[23] What has changed is that Khan and others are using the power of the Reputation Economy to make something new of distance education: a *verifiable, creditable model* that can succeed in disrupting much of traditional higher education where early self-directed online learning models have struggled.

In other words, what makes the Khan Academy—and other start-ups like it—truly valuable and revolutionary isn't the massive library of online videos (thousands of hours), the celebrity endorsers (LeBron James), or even the cost (free)—but the ecosystem of credentialing that is quickly evolving around it. Khan envisions "microcredentials"—he believes that instead of being granted one college diploma at the end of four or more years, people should be able to be tested in as many or as few disciplines as they want—and not just what they learned in the classroom either.[24] Work an internship in a museum, then take a test for a credential in museum studies. Take a series of classes in computer science, then take a practical exam in that field for a credential. And so on. Seem futuristic? A consortium of universities you may have heard of—Harvard, MIT, and University of California–Berkeley are already trying it through a program called edX, which issues microcredentials for passing individual online courses. Admittedly, the courses themselves are fairly traditional, but unlike most courses at elite universities they are open to anyone who wants to sign up, not just matriculated students, and they allow people to jump straight to the most advanced courses if they have gained the fundamentals through other means. It's not perfect yet, but it's a start.

A system that provides proof of completion of certain learning (like a microcredential) regardless of where that learning takes place is a necessary step toward using distance learning as a signal in the Reputation Economy, but it is not enough to truly revolutionize the way students are taught and hired. Instead, the real revolution in how education affects the hiring process will come when employers are able to evaluate students as they graduate using the one criterion that matters: whether they will make good employees in *this particular job, at this particular company.*

One company, EmployInsight, is trying to fill part of that gap. Instead of evaluating students on the basis of their academic records (been there, done that), applicants take an online test that in many ways resembles a personality test, or even the sort of questions you might see on dating sites like eHarmony. From their responses EmployInsight rates each candidate on character traits like "authenticity," "gratitude," and "creativity," then uses algorithms to try to match candidates with the best jobs for them.

EmployInsight is not alone in using data-driven methods to evaluate candidates. Employee evaluation has become a hot area within the tech sector, drawing multibillion-dollar investments. In 2012, for example, database giant Oracle acquired Taleo Corporation for $1.9 *billion* in order to add to its enterprise offerings the Taleo Cloud service, which allows hiring managers to cost-effectively screen a larger number of candidates than previously possible. If it's possible to offer a work-sample test to one hundred candidates for the same price as interviewing ten plucked on the basis of their college degrees, the hiring game changes dramatically. Suddenly, that faded sheepskin has become even less relevant and actual job skills have become more so.

Of course, no employment screening system or algorithm is able to perfectly predict job performance—yet. But if baseball statisticians can predict player performance through analytics like Sabermetrics, which allows baseball fans to predict exactly how many wins a star will ratchet up for his team (the so-called VORP, or value over replacement player), the ability to predict job performance is not far behind.[25] And Sabermetrics was created largely for free, so imagine what literally billions of dollars of investment in the field of employment screening will do: it can't be long before a machine will be able to say, "This candidate will make $10,000 more in sales per month than your average current employee"—a sort of VORP score for business.

Just as baseball players who don't fit traditional expectations have been promoted thanks to new forms of analysis (like Kevin Youkilis, whom one writer described as looking less like a player than like "a refrigerator repairman, a butcher, the man selling hammers behind the counter at the True Value hardware store"—and who went on to three All-Star games and two world championships), the same will soon be true of individual professionals.[26] This will be the time for nontraditional students and people with circuitous life paths to shine. Even if you didn't go to the top school in your field—or even if you didn't have a conventional education at all, for that matter—increasingly personalized scoring will give you the chance to prove you can deliver the goods at the end of the day. And our strong prediction is that, over time, it will become clear that nontraditional credentials and life stories will be worth a lot more than they get credit for now.

One More College Try

Just because the Reputation Economy offers a better way of identifying talent doesn't mean it will be instantly adopted. To paraphrase introductory physics, a system at rest tends to stay at rest, and getting companies and employers to abandon their long-held reliance on the signaling mechanisms of higher education won't be easy. But luckily there is a unique motivating force for change: the aforementioned rapid increase in total student debt and the cost of higher education. Right now, students tolerate an astounding amount of administrative inefficiency—professors with low class loads, graduate students researching arcane topics being subsidized by undergraduate tuition, and so on—in part because they are able to justify it by the value of signaling. In other words, people are willing to put up with high college tuition because they need the signaling *and* education aspects of it. Practically every high school senior in the country is reminded that the lifetime earning potential of college graduates is currently estimated to be $1 million higher than that of high school graduates.[27] Even though the *education* role of college is responsible for only a fraction of that $1 million (as we've seen, the rest comes from the signaling value of college), if you are paying the same institution to provide both, the distinction hardly matters. As a result, colleges are able to increase enrollment, tuition, public funding, and donations by trumpeting that increased lifetime value.

One can see why universities will fight losing their dual role as educator and signaler by resisting any efforts to reduce employers' and recruiters' reliance on GPAs and diplomas. In fact, universities may redouble their efforts to block employers from using reputation scores (calculated from things other than GPAs) because external reputation scores threaten the business model of the university by undermining the ability of the university to extract signaling value. Universities can get away with charging so much in part because they are the gatekeeper to many good jobs, even if many schools don't actually teach the skills required for those jobs. Students complain about the high cost of tuition, but if an investment of $100,000 today will return $1 million over a lifetime, the choice is clear *so long as there is no better alternative.* The Reputation Economy creates that better alternative.

Over time, colleges will have to respond by grading and ranking in more meaningful ways. Already, some schools like Stanford and MIT, which tend to produce entrepreneurs who work outside the traditional hiring system, are evaluating students by criteria other than traditional test scores, and soon other colleges will follow suit by testing students on more of the practical hard skills that employers increasingly demand.

That's not to say that the future of education will be entirely a vo-tech world; well-rounded students on average do better in jobs and life. But philosophy majors will have to demonstrate some additional skills—demonstrating practical learning in addition to their philosophy background will be a great way to show that they can immerse themselves in an area and study hard. Similarly, social skills will increasingly be evaluated; after all, one of the key assets to an employer is the ability to get along, work on teams, and lead when appropriate.

Thanks to advances in data analytics, credentials in these areas can easily become tangible and measurable to an employer. Instead of minoring in computer science, imagine taking an edX course at the apex of the computer science curriculum and earning a certificate from it with high honors—despite being largely self-taught. Plenty of good employers will accept the edX certificate and consider it to be as meaningful as a state college minor. The same goes for a portfolio piece in any field—we discussed engineers using a start-up company as a portfolio piece of sorts, but a standout piece of journalism, a business case study, or a speaking gig can do the same in other fields.

So if you are a student or graduate who has followed traditional educational models, consider investing in some rigorous courses outside your field—particularly when applied to practical topics. There's no need for every class to be exactly business-relevant (if you're a marketing major, you should still take English literature and poetry and foreign languages and film), but let's just say that the ability to quote passages from *Henry VIII* or compare the teachings of Greek philosophers is a much less valued signal to employers than it once was. Indeed, as the Reputation Economy grows, candidates will be increasingly judged by the *variety and rigor* of their course loads. A candidate who excels despite a difficult set of classes will be doubly praised: first for excelling and second for having the motivation to challenge herself to take difficult classes (and employers will know which classes are difficult; even today sites like RateMyProfessors assign publicly visible difficulty scores to individual classes). At the same time, experiences gained outside the academy are increasing in value. Technical skills (such as computer programming) will be the first to be scored; they are more easily quantified than "soft skills" (such as management and people skills), and even stodgy employers believe that technical skills can be self-taught. Later, increasingly soft skills will become testable outside the academy, empowering students to self-educate in those areas as well.

That said, it's not clear that walking away from college is a wise decision for most students. College has a long way to go before the sheepskin effect disappears entirely. Even Silicon Valley entrepreneur Peter Thiel—one of the most vocal champions of nontraditional learning, to the point where he started a fellowship that awards twenty-four students $100,000 each to drop out of college and start companies—has cut back his public opposition to college. And top schools—the Dukes, Harvards, Stanfords, and MITs of the world—will be a great bet for a long time; they are still a very strong signal of a good education (plus invaluable for networking) that will not be displaced for many years. So don't look for a large drop-off in applications to Yale and Harvard the year after this book comes out; as in many things, the top 1 percent of schools will find ways to prosper.

Smart students and job seekers will combine traditional *and* nontraditional elements of their educations. Not only does this make you a more attractive candidate to employers, it's also cheaper and more practical. If you can learn technical skills outside the classroom (and receive relevant credentials and certifications of those skills) through free or reduced-cost online learning, you can either graduate faster (and save both cash tuition and the opportunity cost of not working) or have more time to focus on the kinds of soft skills (teamwork, presentations, creativity, etc.) that are difficult to measure through online exams (or both). The Reputation Economy makes this possible by making it easier to measure relevant skills without all the baggage that comes with the full college experience.

For example, several online education companies and organizations are very close to presenting thorough curricula that integrate with traditional schools. For example, a student could use an online education service to pick up the technical skill set of an MBA (such as accounting, finance, and statistics) as a complement to a traditional MBA curriculum focused on the soft skills required of the role (leadership, teamwork, presentations, management, etc.). These combination programs will have credential value too, so long as they are adequately rigorous; the point isn't that higher education will lose all its value but that it will no longer be the *only* way to recognize talent.

No matter what field you are in, you can strengthen your position by learning as much as possible in areas that can be quantified and tested. The most easily testable areas will be hard sciences and math, followed by vocational skills that can be tested digitally and other occupational skills. (There's already a prostate exam simulator for testing the skills of radiology technicians. It comes with a 3D plastic component and software that simulates the "patient's" reaction on a nearby computer screen—miss a section of the prostate and the computer will score you lower; apply too much pressure and the virtual patient will loudly complain about it.)[28] Business students and MBAs are likely to be among the last to undergo automated testing; they may be tested for subjects such as accounting, compliance, and operations, but much of the MBA curriculum covers soft skills like negotiating and leadership that do not yet digitize well. Lawyers will be somewhere in the middle: there already is a notorious state-run credentialing exam, and some states allow people to take the bar exam without having a law degree or ever going to law school. But other states are more protective of the legal guild and will crack down even further if too many students are able to enter the profession without following traditional paths. If you're a doctor, the news is good or bad depending on your perspective: no matter how accurate scoring algorithms become, it will be many decades before any state allows a doctor to practice medicine without a medical degree—no matter what scores that person has gotten or how likely it is that he or she will be a good doctor. But that doesn't mean doctors are immune—once you enter practice, reputation scoring and grading will dramatically change how patients and payers (insurers and employers) view you. You will no longer be able to rely on your white coat as the ultimate credential; instead, your practice will be observed and measured every day, with possibly dramatic results to your compensation.

The short version of the story is this: In a world where predictions about your future job performance are increasingly made by computers, your ability to demonstrate the value of your education in actual skills will be far more valuable than the traditional signals of a high GPA and a fancy sheepskin. In a DAMM world, racking up as many credentials as possible that can be digitized, quantified, and measured will be crucial to launching a successful career in any field.

7

Instant

Live Like a VIP in a Reputation
Economy World

I N THE REPUTATION ECONOMY, NOT ONLY WILL MOST OF your interactions with other people and businesses affect your balance of reputation capital, but these interactions will be reflected in your reputation score instantly. A surprise compliment from your boss will instantly increase it; an intemperate Facebook comment will instantly lower it. Return a rental car dirty in the morning, and by afternoon your ability to rent an apartment will suffer. Do an unexpected good deed in the afternoon, and by evening you'll be getting a special upgrade to first class that feels like karma (but might really be just a cold computer calculation of your do-good score and a shameless attempt by a corporation to cash in on your goodwill).

And while reputation information is becoming more instantly

available, it is also becoming more public and transparent. This means not only that will companies and businesses have access to instant real-time information about you but that you'll also have instant access to real-time reputation data for the businesses and people you interact with. At a restaurant, one rude waiter, cold entrée, or warm beer served to another patron may be all it takes for the establishment's reputation to plunge—and you will have instant and real-time access to that information through your smartphone, or maybe even your smart glasses.

It's a transparent world and we're all just living in it.

Instant Updates, Always Available

One of the first online advertisements for Google's Glass project—for the uninitiated, a set of eyeglasses with a tiny display and a video camera embedded in the frame—was a YouTube video showing a first-person view of what a typical day with Google Glass might be. Despite the sci-fi nature of having an always-on video screen centimeters from your eyeballs, the ad tries to show the experience of using Glass as normal and unobtrusive. The commercial is shot from the perspective of a Glass user walking down a New York City street wearing the device. As the Glass user walks, he sees business information (like a map of the inside of the nearby Strand bookstore) automatically pop up in his field of view. As he walks past the entrance to the subway, he sees schedule updates (that his subway line is temporarily closed). The result is a sort of "pop-up video" for the real world—information about everything around you appears right in your field of vision. And all of this data is, the advertisement implies, sourced in real time: any updates are accessible literally at a glance into a set of Google Glass spectacles.[1]

Thankfully (at least as of this writing), Google Glass has failed to reach the mainstream, and we have not yet turned into a nation of camera-wearing cyborgs. But the point is that in much the same way that the Google search can deliver real-time updates about everything from restaurant reservations, to flight delays, to the latest sale at the Gap, so can reputation engines deliver real-time reputation updates to your smartphone, your tablet, or any number of other mobile (or stationary) devices.

Know Your Reputation Capital Balance Anytime

It's hard to believe today, but there was actually a time when it wasn't possible to check your bank or credit card or brokerage account balance online. In fact, just a short decade ago it was a major pain to check the balance of an account in between monthly or quarterly statements. Before the days of mobile or even Internet banking, there was a time when customers had to visit actual bank branches (and of course most banks were only open "Monday through Friday, 9:00 a.m. to 4:00 p.m.," and sometimes for even shorter hours) if they needed to know their account balance or make a transaction. But today, most transactions can be done from home in your underclothes; we can make deposits, check our balance, and transfer cash with a single swipe on our smartphone (with my bank, I'm only a text message away from instantly receiving my account balance, 24/7/365, and an increasing number of banks even allow customers to make deposits by taking cell phone photos of checks). In fact, banks like Capital One 360 and Ally Bank have largely done away with branches entirely—Capital One 360 runs a few "cafés" (more like coffee shops than banks, without most banking services), and Ally has only corporate offices.

Just as banking information has gone from being infrequently updated and available only at inconvenient times to instant and always available, the same is about to happen with reputation information. Right now, your balance of reputation capital is inconvenient and hard to compute: it is spread across a variety of sources—your credit score, your driving record, your "host rating" on Airbnb—that are updated at different times and with differing degrees of visibility. Your reputation capital can already be accessed and estimated, but it is not instant, online, and accessible at a fingertip in a convenient and easy-to-interpret formula. However, that is all soon to change.

The same goes for reputation information about others. Right now, it is still somewhat time-consuming to assemble a snapshot of somebody else's reputation—even with the subject's permission. That's not to say that there isn't already a fire hose of information available. But the information is scattered across a variety of sources with varying degrees of reliability, relevance, and accessibility. It takes a computer and time to track it all down to build a profile of one person.

But this is all changing rapidly too. To start with, there are now plenty of tools that provide instant, real-time information about people around you. And of course, this works both ways. Just as the information about others is available to *you* at any time, so is the information about you available to anyone who wants it. There's a reason that CNN and other full-time news networks exist: some people enjoy receiving a steady flow of information, and the Internet is more than happy to provide it. But instead of getting hooked on CNN or CNBC, you can get hooked on data about your friends, coworkers, bosses, classmates—whatever group matters the most to you. And just as you can now get real-time updates about the war in Syria (or wherever today's hot spot is), the latest dip in the markets, and the score of the Red Sox game, soon you'll be able to get real-time reputation updates about other people and things, and they will be able to get real-time updates about you as well.

As just one example, the Girls Around Me app quite literally sends your smartphone a list of women who have recently used Facebook's "check-in" feature at any bar in your proximity. We're not suggesting this type of app is groundbreaking or even socially desirable; we are simply demonstrating that the technology exists. For now, the app provides very little in the way of reputation information: it doesn't even attempt to identify which women are plausible romantic matches (whether as "Mrs. Right" or "Ms. Right Now"), for example, but this feature will surely be built into future versions. (In the interest of neutrality, the app Grindr offers a similar service to men looking for other men that adds profiles but still precious little other information. If there ever is a "Grindr 2.0"—and the odds are good that there will be—it will be a prime candidate to add reputation information about everything from wealth to the satisfaction reported by Grindr partners.)

Other apps are slowly helping bridge the reputation information gap in more constructive ways. For example, the app MedXSafe allows users to (with each other's permission and consent) "bump" their phones together in order to get each other's instant, verified STD test results (entered through a certified physician platform)—thus allowing people to ascertain their potential partner's health status before they do any bumping of their own.[2] The app Strava allows users to compete against each other in running, cycling, and other sports by comparing times across the same course—your friend runs the hill course on Monday and you try to beat her time on Tuesday, all within your iPhone or Android device. Top runners and cyclists develop a reputation (complete with scores and badges) that they can then use to brag to others, while presumably getting fitter in the process.

These small apps are a stepping-stone toward a world where all it takes to get troves of information about somebody is a smartphone photo—or just a glance with a Google Glass camera. Facial recognition (especially if guided by location, friends, or other facts) is becoming increasingly powerful and will lead to dramatic results when combined with Reputation Economy–style data analysis. Imagine that when you walk into a car dealership the sales staff instantly know your approximate wealth based on the value of your house and when you bought it (via facial recognition and public property records). Or imagine that when you walk into a bar three people of the opposite sex instantly turn away from you after your dating score plunges thanks to a scathing online review from a previous significant other. You get the idea—your reputation will be used publicly, instantly, whether you like it or not.

On Demand, Not in Your Face

The instant nature of the new Reputation Economy doesn't mean we'll constantly be bombarded with updates; after all, just because technology exists to deliver a constant, real-time stream of information doesn't mean we have to pay attention to it. Most of us won't opt into messages like "Your boss is up 2 points this morning" or "Your favorite lunch restaurant lost 1 point for serving cold soup at 11:30 a.m. today." The point is that just like your bank balance, the information will be constantly updated behind the scenes and made available to you whenever you want or need it.

A Two-Way Street

In the pre–Reputation Economy days, reputation information about businesses flowed primarily one direction—to the consumer. For example, any individual looking to book a hotel or choose a restaurant or find a used car dealership could go on Yelp or Angie's List or TripAdvisor for information on that establishment's reputation, but your local steak-and-potatoes restaurant had no way to look up its customers as they walked in the door. But today, thanks to the explosion of peer-to-peer services like Airbnb, RelayRides, and Lyft, both customers *and* service providers can access reputation information about one another. Take the room-sharing service Airbnb, for example. In some ways this service works like a hotel: hosts can rent out a house, an apartment, a room, or even just a futon on a nightly basis. Just as with a traditional hotel, customers pick a host and request a reservation, and afterward they can review their hosts and the quality of their experiences. But here's the twist. The hosts, unlike the managers of a traditional hotel, can also review their guests. It may be a long time before the local Holiday Inn posts online reviews of its customers, but the growing popularity of Airbnb and other peer-to-peer services demonstrates that we are soon heading for a world where ratings of *you* as a hotel guest or a restaurant patron or an apartment tenant will be public, instantly available, and, as we've seen in previous chapters, indelible.

Examples of individual digital reputation scoring—with personal and commercial consequences—are emerging quickly. For one, Airbnb has begun to allow landlords to evaluate their renters on how clean, tidy, respectful, and congenial they have been during or at the end of their stays.[3] The ramifications of this are obvious: prospective guests who enjoy good digital reputations on Airbnb will likely soon enjoy lower prices, diminished or disappeared down payments and deposits, and other privileges.

Businesses have always shared secret (and controversial) blacklists, but they were relatively closed: for example, Las Vegas casino security is notorious for keeping a list of forbidden customers who are banned across several hotels. But the list has never been shared or made public; it's not as if you are at risk of being kicked out of the Olive Garden just because you're no longer welcome at Applebee's (let alone Mandalay Bay). But that's all changing in the world of instant, public, two-way feedback between consumers and service providers. Get blacklisted from Airbnb, and other services may follow as well; publicly complain about it, and your reputation might suffer even further.

The same trend is appearing in the restaurant business. OpenTable, perhaps the best-known restaurant reservation tool in the United States, has blocked users from making reservations on its site when the users have had too many no-shows.[4] If you make reservations you don't keep, you risk getting flagged by restaurants as a bad customer. Too many such reports, and you get kicked off the island and lose your reservation privileges.

But on the flip side of that coin, the two-way flow of reputation information can yield many benefits. For example, imagine that you walk into an outpost of your favorite Italian chain restaurant. It's the first time you've ever visited this particular branch—in fact, it's the first time you've ever been to this city. But as soon as you give your name at the host stand, you and your party are escorted directly to a table (even though you never made reservations) and are offered a complimentary aperitif. The waiter reads the specials of the day, offers two extra vegetarian options (How did he know you recently gave up meat?), and brings you complimentary sparkling water instead of tap (your preference). In other words, you get instant VIP status based solely on your reputation as a good tipper and a loyal customer—and because the restaurant can easily access records of what you've ordered on previous occasions (if they wish), your experience is instantly customized to your preferences. This is the difference between a world in which information about you merely exists and one in which it can be easily accessed. In the pre–Reputation Economy world, a maître d' could theoretically find out what you ordered at your last gourmet dining experience—but it would probably take a series of phone calls and a whole lot of time and effort. Today, that information is stored in a database that that maître d' can instantly access if he wishes—but he'll do it only for those patrons with favorable reputations. Build a reputation as a good customer, and you'll get preferential treatment not just at one restaurant but at others. Free appetizer, a complimentary dessert, a short pressure-point shoulder massage. Who knows? But clearly the goods will come to the ones with the best digital reputations.

Whether you're a VIP at a local watering hole, a midmarket chain, or a five-star restaurant, in today's Reputation Economy if you're somebody's best customer, you'll be rewarded for it. Seem futuristic? An application called Facedeals already offers customized offers based on facial recognition at merchant doorways, culled from your Facebook profile—as you walk in, you get a text with an offer if you're a favored customer (or not, if not).[5] Creepy or clever? Probably both, but plenty of people are willing to feel like VIPs at the price of their privacy.

The world of air travel has long operated according to a similar VIP rewards system, but thanks to the technologies that allow for greater sharing of reputation information, this system is about to get a whole lot more complicated. Today any business traveler worth her roll-aboard bag is a member of at least one frequent flier program—and maybe more.

But airlines don't offer these rewards programs out of the goodness of their hearts. Instead, these programs have at least two business goals: to encourage loyalty and to identify frequent travelers for whom offering special treatment might result in more—and more lucrative—business (especially if they are traveling on a work expense account and can pay higher average fares than leisure travelers). It's a win-win situation for both the airlines and the travelers who are rewarded with the free airfares and special status.

But there has always been a tension: If you are a marketing director at United Airlines, how do you go about luring a flier who already has some elite rewards status with American Airlines? (On the basis of our exposure to boarding announcements, it seems as though the programs are running out of rare metals and gemstones after which to name their programs.) Suddenly, the incentives have become misaligned: a serious business traveler might represent $10,000 in annual revenue to United, so United definitely has an incentive to try to poach her from American. But the flier has no incentive to switch: she already gets elite boarding privileges from American and would have to start over with United—go back to boarding the plane with the common vacation traveler, no longer getting lounge access? No thanks.

The solution is a dirty and well-kept secret of frequent flier programs called status matching. The major carriers each have a different policy but will in general automatically match elite statuses with each other: in other words, if you can show that you have a high enough status with a competing carrier, it is often possible to get at least temporary elite status with another. But, like the blacklists at Vegas casinos, the rules of the matching programs—which airlines are eligible for matching, what level of elite status must be shown to be matched, and so forth—are not yet public or transparent and change frequently. But that's also part of the problem: the more complex it is to try to get matching, the more dedicated a flier has to be in order to seek it out. So if you're a marketing director at United, how do you identify and lure people who are feeling borderline about American?

The Reputation Economy provides the solution to this conundrum. In the future, airlines will be able to instantly figure out which travelers are *likely* to be frequent business travelers and to proactively lure them with better offers and more elite status. But how can these airlines predict which travelers have the *potential* to fly more frequently and at higher fares? Through computer algorithms programmed to scan customers' digital footprints for certain tells. A change in a LinkedIn status from "inside sales rep" to "field sales rep" might be enough: top field sales teams can travel hundreds of thousands of air miles per year. The same goes for an update about a promotion from junior to senior executive, or a new job at a global business, both of which are likely to confer more travel—and bigger expense accounts. Even just a sharp increase in Foursquare check-ins or Facebook statuses from different cities around the country might be enough to predict a future uptick in travel and prompt an airline to offer you special status and perks not being offered to other passengers.

As the Reputation Economy matures, companies will hone their predictive analysis even further. Instead of simply judging how likely you are to travel, a second-generation program will look at your reputation for loyalty to other types of businesses and subtly adjust your program rewards accordingly. For example, if you always stop at the same coffee shop on the way to work, if you order the same dish for dinner every Friday, and if your last three cars have been from the same manufacturer, you'll get a high loyalty score, and in turn you'll be more heavily courted by all other types of businesses—at least initially. The downside is that in time you may find that the level and quality of service decrease after that initial lovefest: after all, if you're so loyal, you aren't the type to require constant attention. By contrast, if you have a low loyalty score (constantly trying new restaurants, buying the new hot car from a different manufacturer every few years, etc.), no prudent carrier would invest a lot to lure you, since you are unlikely to stay with them. But they might offer smaller perks—maybe a seat upgrade or free standby on an earlier flight—just enough to get you to complete a particular transaction with them. In the Reputation Economy, this can all take place instantly: a computer will automatically check your reputation when you buy a ticket or check in, and within seconds (no more time than it takes to print a boarding pass or process a credit card transaction) decide whether you deserve these perks. It doesn't take an application form, an interview, or personal research—it all takes place in the blink of an eye. And this information can be updated in a blink as well—get a promotion in the morning and you may be upgraded on your afternoon flight, perhaps even before your family knows the good news. (Retail chain Target once "outed" someone in this dramatic fashion, sending a packet of "congratulations on your pregnancy" coupons to a teen mother who had not yet told her family the news.)[6]

And of course airlines won't be the only ones to implement these kinds of practices. Banks, hotel chains, car dealerships, real estate companies—anyone competing for your business— will be increasingly reviewing, analyzing, and parsing your reputation scores in myriad ways that will determine what kinds of perks, deals, and offers you are offered—and that you don't even realize are passing you over.

So if you want to chase as many perks as possible, keep your online profile updated and accurate. It's hard to fake travel check-ins (most sites verify your location with GPS or other technologies), but it is very easy to publicize your travel (preferably after you're back, so as to not entice burglars). Don't be shy about checking into your airports and destinations; flaunt your road warrior status and make sure the Internet knows you're the next *Up in the Air*. More generally, publicize promotions and increases in your status—it's not just airlines that are looking for high rollers. Promptly update your LinkedIn or other professional profile with the good news, and make sure your upward arc is visible. And there's nothing wrong with publicizing what you're shopping for; consider tweets like "Looking for new SUV, considering @BMWUSA or @MBUSA, any experiences?" or "Considering moving to private bank, anyone have suggestions?" While it's far from guaranteed, these sorts of public statements may attract the attention of computers searching for people who can be encouraged to jump at a good bargain. Even better, make sure it's clear you're on the fence—if you're already committed to one brand, they have no reason to approach you.

Another good tactic is to celebrate the brands that you really love. If you have a positive experience with a brand, tweet it or put it on your Facebook: "Great service @BofA_Help today—I messed up my direct deposit form, but manager Cindy was able to get it straightened out in just 10 minutes." Same for products that you love: "Loving my #newcar. It gets 100 miles #allelectric but it drives like a sportscar." Being positive and public about your likes will give you a reputation as a social influencer—and brands will drool to get your business, especially if you have a large number of followers. If an airline sees your brags about your bank, for example, they may hope to get similar public praise from you if they can lure you with special offers and lounge access.

"What Have You Done for AmEx Lately?"

Most major credit cards offer a very pre–Reputation Economy deal: they give you a fixed credit limit that allows customers to keep up to a certain balance at any time. Most legacy issuers update that maximum balance infrequently: when the user misses a payment or calls to request an increase, or as part of a periodic (annual or semiannual) review.

By contrast, American Express has always advertised the fact that its card members (their term) do not have fixed credit limits. Of course, that doesn't mean you could apply for an American Express card today and use it to buy a Bentley tomorrow; "no *fixed* limit" doesn't mean "no limit." Most credit card companies look only at your credit limit and recent payment history when deciding to authorize a charge. If you haven't reached your limit, the transaction will be authorized; if you go over the limit, they may still authorize the transaction if you have generally paid your bill recently (but they may charge you between $20 and $50 as an over-limit fee). But American Express, instead of authorizing a transaction on the basis of whether you've reached your credit limit, has its sophisticated computer system analyze each particular transaction on the basis of the card member's history, the card member's recent transactions, the company's experiences with other card members who have made similar transactions, market trends, and other data—in other words, it tries to make decisions about your credit on the basis of your reputation and the behavior of those who have preceded you. If the computer thinks American Express is likely to be paid back, it authorizes the transaction; if the transaction raises a red flag, it may deny the transaction or request manual review. Most people are happy with the system—in general, it seems that most good charges go through. But the risk many people face is that one major hit to their reputation can cause a cascading collapse of their financial means: accidentally go over your credit limit, and all of a sudden AmEx and other lenders pull the plug on charges, turning a speed bump into a mountain of trouble.

The American Express model represents the future of credit. In the old model, a credit limit established years ago—often back when you opened an account—determines what credit you'll be offered, but in the Reputation Economy your credit-worthiness is being constantly and instantly updated. Get a raise? Your credit will be instantly increased to reflect it. Win a major client at work? The same: even if winning the major client doesn't directly lead to a raise or a bonus, it is further evidence that you have high potential and you will find a way to succeed, so the reputation engines may factor in this information. Lenders and credit card companies will analyze this data and offer bigger credit limits and better reward points for upwardly mobile professionals—giving them a competitive advantage and leaving the less mobile consumers for their competitors.

Unfortunately, the same effect on credit will be true for negative events as well. Did you make an offensive comment about your boss on Facebook? While no credit card company would admit to factoring in this information, you can see how it might easily be used as a reason to reduce your credit limit: if you get fired, any card that doesn't instantly reduce your credit will be left with a big balance when you suddenly can't make your payments. True, most derogatory comments do not lead to any work discipline at all, but they are still a sign of increased risk:

that you are prone to other behavior that *could* lead to a job loss directly or that you may be dissatisfied enough with your job to resign. Of course, the point is not whether bashing your boss on Facebook will lead to unemployment but the fact credit card companies—and banks and lenders and anyone else—can easily and instantly access records of all your online activity and use it as criteria to offer or deny you credit. Worse, the result will be automated; obviously there are no rooms filled with AmEx employees carefully scrutinizing every Facebook post. Instead, this work is being done by computers that lack a sense of humor, a sense of context, or compassion and that automatically scan and come up with a "sentiment analysis" (a computer's guess as to whether a text is emotionally positive or negative) to create scores.

Other important decisions that affect your finances have been made completely instant and automatic as well. Take, for example, online payments. In the early years of the online payment company PayPal, fraudulent charges were costing the company more than $10 million per month during a period when its total revenue from fees was less than $5 million per month.[7] In other words, PayPal was losing money to fraud more than twice as fast as it was making money. The company was bound for bankruptcy just on the basis of the amount of fraud.

In response, a team at PayPal built a network of computers that could analyze every transaction and block or reject each on the basis of the computer's analysis of whether the transaction was fraudulent. The system took into account thousands of factors, ranging from the size of the transaction, to the IP addresses of the sender and the recipient, to previous experiences with the sender and the recipient, to the number and similarity of other transfers happening (in seemingly unrelated accounts) at the same time. Simultaneously, another layer of computers analyzed groups of transactions to determine whether any particular account was likely to be used for fraud or whether scammers were trying to hide fraudulent transactions in batches of legitimate transactions. Within seconds, the computers could automatically reject individual transactions or shut down entire accounts, in some cases blocking access to funds entirely without human interaction.

The system has successfully stopped the organized fraud that nearly destroyed early PayPal, but at a cost. Merchants and individuals began to complain that the computer shut down their legitimate account, freezing important funds in the process. Some victims of erroneous decisions to ban their accounts reported that contacting a human at PayPal to appeal the decision was futile. In the Reputation Economy, decisions like this are made instantly and automatically, and once they are made they often can't be reversed.

PayPal is far from the only company managing important transactions by using the power of instant computer decision making. Take short-term lenders, particularly "payday" lenders who give loans without taking any collateral (unlike pawnshop loans or car title loans). People who use payday lenders are almost by definition not good candidates for traditional credit; they are often at the edge of their financial means, trying to make ends meet until the next paycheck comes in.

Most borrowers walk into a storefront payday loan office and show a paystub to a cashier, who will make a loan from as little as $50 to as much as $1,000. Very few questions are asked; the application form often fits on the front of a single page, and the loan agreement takes just a few more. More recently, many payday lenders have taken the same process online. Nearly everyone qualifies, but at interest rates that would make a banker blush. It's highly controversial, but it is a huge sector that expanded dramatically during the financial slowdown of the late 2000s to early 2010s.

Payday lending effectively fills the demand for a type of loan that fits between bank lending (where loans are usually awarded at an individual banker's discretion and thus are subject to bias) and loan sharking (which is often shady and controlled by organized crime), but payday lenders face a costly problem: their willingness to lend to nearly any customer results in a high default rate. One of the largest payday lenders, Cash America, for example, issues about $3 billion in loans a year but writes off more than $225 million in what it calls "consumer loss," which is just a polite term for debtors who take out loans and never pay them back.[8] And a report sponsored by the U.S. government found that an average of 15 percent of payday loans go unpaid, and that the percentage is even higher in some markets.[9]

In 2006, British entrepreneurs Errol Damelin and Jonty Hurwitz saw this abysmal 15 percent loss rate and thought, "We can do better." They sought to combine the accuracy of a banker with the speed and convenience of a payday lender by using computers (rather than bankers) to analyze the reputations of short-term borrowers and identify which were most likely to pay.

By using a computer to select only the best-quality borrowers, Damelin and Hurwitz suggested, lenders would be able to reduce their expenses, offer lower fees and better customer service, and still make more money than traditional paystub lenders. So they set out to write a mathematical formula that would predict who would pay and who would default by analyzing thousands of data points (rumored to include housing information, Web searches for customers' names, and maybe even genealogy databases) and comparing them to previous applicants who paid their loan on time to those who failed to do so.[10]

Damelin and Hurwitz assumed it would be easy to raise funds for such a venture, especially given that they were both already successful entrepreneurs. But, ironically, traditional banks laughed them out of the room, just as they did to payday borrowers. Eventually, they found funding and launched under the name Wonga. Within minutes, the first customer applied for a loan, and within a week a customer defaulted. In other words, they found out within just seven days that their algorithm was far from perfect and paid a financial price for the lesson. But they didn't give up. Over time, their algorithm gradually refined itself by learning from these failures, and the Wonga model began to pay off. Now the algorithm rejects two-thirds of applicants and Wonga is below a 10 percent loss rate—still higher than bank loans, but 33 percent lower than the short-term lending industry standard of 15 percent. And, paradoxically, Wonga reports that its customers are happier too; Wonga claims that 91 percent of customers who have used multiple short-term lenders prefer Wonga.

One further result of Wonga's success is that payday lenders that *don't* use data-driven methods like Wonga face even higher costs; Wonga is able to select "good" borrowers who are likely to repay and leave the lesser borrowers to traditional payday lenders. As Wonga skims more and more of the cream off the top of the payday lending market, traditional payday lenders will have to raise their fees higher and higher to cover increasingly low-quality lending candidates. A vicious circle will follow: the higher the rates charged by payday lenders, the more borrowers will apply first at Wonga, and the fewer high-quality borrowers will be left for traditional payday lenders, causing traditional payday lenders to have to increase rates yet again. The eventual result may be the end of the payday loan as we know it, to be replaced by reputation-based lending customized for each borrower.

As predictive models like these become more sophisticated, they will become even more difficult to fool. With huge amounts of money on the line, many lenders are looking for reasons to disqualify you rather than reasons to lend to you. Just as for other reputation scores, avoid public spats with your boss or any other behavior that might indicate you are about to quit or get fired. Also, remember that banks and others look at your friends to determine what kind of risk you will be, so if you are deep in the process of trying to take out a large loan (such as a mortgage), avoid unnecessarily publicizing your relationship with anyone who has recently declared bankruptcy or been foreclosed on. And at the risk of seeming cynical, it wouldn't hurt to "friend" a few people who have recently come into a windfall or earned a big raise. The more you can make it appear *to a computer* that you hobnob with financially well-off individuals, the higher your scores are likely to be.

The Fallibility of Instant

To put it bluntly, systems in which rewards are meted out on the basis of real-time reputation scoring work great, until they don't. In other words, most of the time trustworthy and responsible behavior will result in instant improvements in reputation scores, and in turn those responsible and trustworthy people will be rewarded with financial perks, special offers, instant VIP status, and other preferred opportunities based on their status. The only problem is that whether through a glitch in the computer algorithm or the acquisition of misinformation, the system will occasionally spin out of control. And because our digital footprints are so lasting and permanent, when it happens there won't be much you can do about it.

Rumor mills on the Internet are not a new phenomenon. Anytime a national tragedy occurs, countless people rush to their computers and begin speculating wildly on their blogs, on Facebook, and on Twitter about the cause of the tragedy. Quickly, some of this speculation begins to be repeated as fact—these days, often by reputable traditional news outlets fearful of getting "scooped" by bloggers and tweeters—and becomes fodder for even wilder speculation. Around it goes until the story becomes completely distorted. Eventually (hopefully) the truth comes out, but usually not until the tangled web of untruths has been unraveled, usually several days later.

As just one example, following the 2013 Boston Marathon bombings a number of online commenters speculated that the bombers were two runners who had been seen holding backpacks near the finish line. Thousands of people across the country then began looking for the same runners in other photos, creating a frenzied pursuit of these two (innocent, as it turned out) people. The crowd even attached a name to one of its suspects: Sunil Tripathi, a Brown University student on leave from the school. It wasn't long before somehow a rumor that Sunil Tripathi "had been identified on a police scanner" became part of the record.[11] Soon, thousands of online amateur detectives were creating dossiers for Sunil Tripathi and his alleged companion, tracing their movements through photos, and speculating as to their motives. The fact that the original question—Is Sunil Tripathi really the suspect?—had never been conclusively answered was lost among questions of "Where is Sunil Tripathi now?" and "Why did Sunil Tripathi do it?"

The online search for Sunil Tripathi spiraled out of control, with some justice seekers going so far as to call his parents' home. Of course, the Chechen brothers Tamerlan and Dzhokhar Tsarnaev were later identified as the actual suspects, and Dzhokhar confessed to police after his capture following a firefight and a citywide manhunt (Tamerlan was killed in his escape attempt). As a sad coda, Sunil Tripathi's body was found in the Providence River about a week later, following a possible suicide.

Of course, this is an extreme example of how a rapidly spreading online rumor can instantly destroy an innocent person's reputation. But while most online rumors don't involve such dramatic events or have such tragic consequences, the mechanism by which they spread and escalate remains the same: initial speculation leads to some incorrect information being accepted as fact, forming the basis for further (false) speculation, as the truth grows more and more distorted with each self-perpetuating cycle. Of course, this has always been true of rumors, but in a world where information—even false information—is made publicly available in an instant, the situation becomes much graver.

In the Reputation Economy, misinformation about you will spread in the blink of an eye, draining your reputation bank account before you even know that there was an error on your balance sheet. Worse yet, in a DAMM world, there are far more opportunities for false or misleading information to take hold; as we've seen, no matter how sophisticated a computer, there are certain ways in which it can never replace a living, breathing human. For example, as discussed in chapters 1 and 3, today, most financial underwriting decisions (such as whether to extend a mortgage loan or a new credit card) are based on what you have done with respect to your finances: the most common FICO score is calculated on the basis of things like whether you have consistently paid your bills and how much credit you have outstanding today. These are all reasonably objective and easily verifiable facts, not usually subject to misinterpretation or error: Did you pay your bill on time or not? How much money do you owe? And so on. But in the Reputation Economy, your financial underwriting will be based on predictions of your financial future, and thus on a more subjective, complicated, and easily misinterpreted set of factors: Do you show career promise? Are you easily fooled or coerced by others? Have you been trustworthy in your dealings with friends? Are you of a moral character that makes you likely to repay your debts?

The risk is that these factors not only are much less objective than those used in traditional credit underwriting but also are subject to the same kind of self-reinforcing cycles as a bad rumor. For example, in the Reputation Economy potential lenders will seek out the most up-to-date information about your career prospects. Thus, if you are a rising star at a growing company you might be offered great credit rates, even if you don't currently make a lot of money or have a long credit history. Sounds great, right? But consider that these predictions are often based on very thin and subjective data: a very small error in some of the input data, like a tweet from a grumpy or disgruntled employee misinterpreted as a sign that your company or division is in trouble (when in fact it is not), can very quickly shake the underwriter's confidence in your prospects, so that suddenly your interest rate skyrockets. Think of it from a lender's perspective: even in a good market, lenders make only a few percent per year on a loan, but a single default can cost them 100 percent of the loan. In other words, the downside risk to a lender is much bigger than the upside. Lenders who are spooked will pull their funding or increase rates at any sign of trouble, even if it later turns out to be nothing.

The problem is amplified by the fact that in a world where

your reputation scores are both public and transparent, this stain on your reputation score will hurt your standing with more than one lender; in today's Reputation Economy lenders and banks are increasingly building the "wisdom of the crowd" into their underwriting decisions. And indeed certain benefits of crowd wisdom have been well established (by now, many people have heard the clichéd story of the contest to guess the weight of an ox at the county fair in which a bunch of experts failed and the most accurate guess came from simply averaging the guesses of hundreds of random passersby). But what happens when the crowd turns into a stampede?

The problem comes, in other words, when all the different businesses and individuals with whom you have relationships—from a landlord trying to verify your desirability as a tenant, to an investor thinking of plunking money into your side business, to a potential employer wondering if you are financially responsible (see how we've come full circle?)—all look to that first lender for information. A self-perpetuating negative cycle can be established very quickly. Or think of what happens if a car rental service like Zipcar, a peer-to-peer housing service like Airbnb, and your bank all look to each other for information about customers. It makes sense for Zipcar to look at a potential renter's Airbnb peer-to-peer housing rental profile to help determine whether a renter is likely to be courteous, prompt, and trustworthy—after all, somebody who treats a rental apartment poorly is also more likely to treat a rental car poorly. The same is also true in reverse: Airbnb has an incentive to find out if its potential housing renters are clean and courteous with respect to rental cars. That's all well and good, but if both were to look only to each other for reputation scores, a self-perpetuating loop would quickly develop: as a user's Zipcar score fell, his Airbnb score would also fall, which would prompt a further decrease in his Zipcar score, and yet another decrease in his Airbnb score . . . you get the idea. Then think of what would happen if your bank or financial underwriter then looked at this same data: a loan might disappear overnight.

Compare this type of feedback loop to traditional FICO credit scoring. For better or for worse, FICO-style credit scoring is heavily regulated and centralized. There is no self-reinforcing bias in FICO scoring; no credit bureau's score is based on any other bureau's score. And, despite all of its flaws, FICO-style credit scoring offers at least some paths toward redress of errors: there are only three credit bureaus that collect credit scoring information and, by law, each must accept certain corrections from consumers. That's not to say that everyone who has been wronged by a FICO score is able to obtain relief. But many consumers are able to correct errors that appear; the slow pace of the system works to protect their reputations from being irreparably harmed.

To protect yourself, take care across *all* areas of your life that might be rated and scored. It wasn't that long ago that if you trashed a hotel room you might be heavily fined by management and banned from that hotel but you would otherwise feel little impact. In the new Reputation Economy, a poor decision in one area of your life—like trashing a hotel room—will be felt across many areas of your life (you'll get a score for it, which may affect your financial and other scores as well). And the same idea holds true for much more modest transgressions. Even little things, like a disagreement with an Airbnb host or a counterparty in an eBay transaction, can escalate into something that will affect scores across the board. Don't let situations like that escalate: if you hit a disagreement, swallow your pride and work it out before it comes back to haunt you.

Equally important is monitoring your data as vigilantly as

you can for errors and mistakes. A sadly common error made by computers continues to be the inability to know the difference between two people with the same name (we'll leave it as an exercise for the reader to figure out which author is still sometimes confused with a college basketball star and frequently gets e-mail intended for many other people who share his name). Monitoring your search results and scores for errors is the only way to catch mistakes before they have become a part of your permanent digital reputation. If you find an error—and by "error" we mean a true error, such as that you weren't actually there or there has been a confusion about your name—take steps immediately to correct it. Explain that it's a *computer error*—not just that you disagree or have additional perspective to add.

After all, in the world where your reputation is as valuable as cash, it's worth the time and effort to monitor it just as you would your bank account or any other asset.

8

Portable

Do NBA Stars Make Good Babysitters?

EBRON JAMES DIDN'T HAVE ANY TROUBLE GETTING A reputation for his skill in the game of basketball. Any fan of the sport knows his name, and any team scout is intimately familiar with his many strengths as a player. Heck, even plenty of people who don't follow the NBA know that he's one of the dominant players of the post-Kobe generation. It doesn't take a fancy computer to know that LeBron would crush nearly any competitor in any variant on basketball, whether played on hardwood, asphalt, or trampolines.

But the NBA championship rings, the MVP trophies, and the rookie-of-the-year award are all irrelevant when it comes to a different question: Should you trust LeBron to babysit your child? Of course, assuming you could extrapolate skill in basketball to skill in babysitting is ridiculous; skill in one area (basketball) does not necessarily correlate with skill in another (babysitting). So how would someone go about judging someone's skill in one area on the basis of his or her reputation in a completely different sphere?

Well, to stick with this (intentionally) ridiculous example, somebody faced with the decision of whether to hire LeBron as a babysitter would start to look beyond the basketball court to other indications of whether he's qualified: like the fact that he has two of his own children, he has additional experience with children from years growing up in the extended household of his coach Frank Walker, he's extremely wealthy (so if he gets in a jam he's likely to have an assistant on speed dial who can look up how to swaddle), and so on. These are extremely limited bits of data to sample from; in reality, very few people would hire a babysitter just on the basis of that information. But before the Reputation Economy world there was simply no way for most people to know much more: all that most people know is that LeBron is one of the top basketball players in the world, and all that a Google search would turn up would be page upon page of basketball stats and highlights.

But imagine a world where it'd be possible to know at a glance whether LeBron James or his Miami teammate Chris Bosh would make a better babysitter. Or, conversely, whether the teenager from down the street whom you hired to watch your kids would grow up to be an NBA star. Or how to parlay your achievements in one field (let's say music) to get a job in another (let's say accounting), no matter where they happened or how seemingly unrelated they were.

The Reputation Economy will bring this form of portability to reputation: what you do today in one skill set, one company, or one area of the world will accrue to your benefit in all areas of your life. Your reputation in one area will spill over to other areas. There are at least three new ways in which your reputation will be "portable." First, your reputation for skill in one field (let's say advertising) will automatically be used as evidence of your skill in related fields (maybe social media marketing). Second, gone will be the days of toiling for years in one position and not having your skills and contributions recognized when you change jobs—your reputation will be portable between jobs to a brand-new extent. Finally, information about your skills and qualifications will become portable across domains as well.

Portability Across Related Skills

The Reputation Economy is all about using data to help people make decisions and predictions with limited secondhand information. If you want to hire a new babysitter, you've probably never seen that person babysit before. And your children are likely to be unique and to present unique challenges to a sitter. So you have no direct way of knowing exactly how well this individual is going to care for your children (and the babysitter has no idea if your children are heaven-sent or little demons). Instead, you have to look to related skills: Is a babysitter candidate generally personable? What experience does he or she have with other people's children? What education? You get the idea. The Reputation Economy will use data to sharpen the focus on which skills are relevant and which are not. From that, individuals will be able to draw sharper conclusions and make better decisions with only second- or thirdhand information.

To stay with Mr. James, it's no secret that he's a gifted overall athlete, and common sense dictates that his prowess at basketball means that he'll likely excel—or at least be much better than the average person—at similar sports. But how far does it go? Would he be an above-average football player? (Almost certainly; there was once even discussion as to whether he should join the NBA or the NFL.) Soccer player? (Maybe. His quickness, stamina, and court presence would likely translate to the game of soccer.) Gymnast? (Probably not. His build is entirely unlike that of most male gymnasts, and he's much too tall.)

It turns out that we no longer have to guess; there is already a data-driven science of predicting the sports in which an athlete will excel, on the basis of a few simple traits (mix of fast- and slow-twitch muscle fibers, reflexes, dominant hand, dominant eye).[1] An athlete with more fast-twitch muscle fibers, great re-flexes, and cross-dominant eyes (e.g., a dominant right hand and a dominant left eye), for example, might be skilled at tennis or baseball. By contrast, other athletes with inferior reflexes but great aerobic capacity (lung and heart capacity) are likely to be strong distance runners or marathoners.

This science allows professional athletic recruiters to make far more precise estimates of an athlete's performance in var-ious sports—and in various levels of play (the science was in-tended, at least, for professional leagues and national Olympic programs, but it has also become yet another obsession for up-wardly mobile parents; a company called Sports X Factor briefly sold a genetic test for parents to identify their child's mix of fast- and slow-twitch muscle fibers, and countless youth sports evaluation facilities have sprung up in affluent neighborhoods). Granted, the market for this is fairly limited, but in the Reputa-tion Economy it will be possible to use these types of analyses beyond the world of athletics to predict how many other types of skills overlap and overflow from one domain to another. One correlation that has received lots of news coverage is that stu-dents who are taught music at a young age end up being, on average, better at math than students who are not exposed to

music.[2] (Of course, averages hold true only across large popula-
tions; it's possible for your "mathlete" nephew to be tone-deaf
or for the most musically gifted person on the planet to fail a
test of simple addition. But if you were forced to pick a high
school student to do a math problem for you, you would at least
be playing the odds correctly if you grabbed the nearest student
carrying a cello or a clarinet.)

It's easy to see the appeal of a method for predicting whether
people who do one thing well are likely to do something else
well. Take an employer looking to hire someone for an entry-
level job that requires math, customer service, and leadership—
maybe a store clerk who has to quickly calculate the correct
amount of change while serving many customers at once. Most
candidates won't have much relevant experience; that's one of
the biggest challenges of hiring people for their first jobs. It's the
classic chicken-and-egg problem: employers want candidates
with experience, but few employers are willing to hire inexperienced people and give them that experience.

To solve that problem, an employer needs a way of identifying the candidates who haven't held a similar job but are still
likely to succeed. For an employer to be willing to take the risk
of hiring untested candidates, the employer must—like the
parents hiring the new babysitter—have some way to separate
the best and worst even without firsthand experience to back it
up. Behavioral interviewing and interviews that simulate actual
work conditions have some validity. But as we've discussed, in
an era where ten job openings can result in thousands of applications, it's impossibly expensive to simulate a test run for each
candidate before narrowing the field.

Instead, the employer needs some method to cherry-pick
promising candidates out of thousands. This is where data analysis methods like those used for athletes come into play. A wise

employer would focus on candidates who have shown skills in other areas (leadership in college or high school activities, success in a previous job, etc.). But how to know which of these is best correlated with the skills the employer wants? By using algorithms based on how well people with similar traits have done in the past. If all the previous employees with experience in, say, accounting have succeeded, you can bet that an accounting certificate will be given special weight.

Take the New York attorney Martin Lipton. Readers who are attorneys will recognize Lipton's name, but most readers won't. And that's part of the point. If you're in the legal or large corporate communities, you know he's a celebrity lawyer. As the "Lipton" of the famous firm Wachtell, Lipton, Rosen & Katz, he literally invented new ways to do corporate transactions, including inventing the "poison pill" in the context of corporate law.

Of course, he's an excellent lawyer. But most people who hire Lipton don't hire him for *his* lawyering. Lipton himself serves hundreds of clients, and simple math suggests that he can't spend more than a few hours on any but the most important accounts. Instead, the younger attorneys he has hired do the vast majority of the work. In other words, people hire Lipton not just for his reputation as a lawyer per se but because they believe the traits that have earned him a reputation as an excellent lawyer have also made him an excellent recruiter and manager. Some of that belief is self-fulfilling: the more people know of his reputation as an excellent lawyer, the more highly qualified younger attorneys will want to work with him. But that's not the whole story; people who hire Lipton quite reasonably assume that his skill in law is so strong that he must also have skill in recruiting and management.

Similarly, many people would trust Mr. Lipton's advice on questions other than pure questions of law. His skills have to be at least two or three standard deviations above average in law, so the assumption goes that he's likely to be at least above average on many other questions (just as LeBron James is so stratospherically better than everyone else at basketball that people figure he must at least be well above average in football or soccer). Given the opportunity, many people would ask his counsel on a broad range of business and ethics questions—ranging from whether a candidate is the right choice for CEO to how to handle tricky relationships with government officials overseas.

But this invites the question: How far does the transferability of his knowledge go? Is he also an expert on computer repair? Would he be a good person from whom to seek relationship advice or religious counsel? Would you want him on your team for pickup basketball?

Before the Reputation Economy, you had no way of knowing. But soon it will be possible for you to look up Martin Lipton (as well as thousands of other professionals) and answer these questions at a glance.

Remember that reputation engines are like search engines that provide a snapshot of a person's reputation by aggregating scores across multiple domains. One reputation engine might focus on legal skills—how many cases a lawyer has argued, how many difficult cases she has won, how many difficult transactions she has helped to close. Yet another might aggregate across different domains, perhaps issuing a friendship score based on the size and strength of the close ties in someone's social network; a charitability score based on his membership in a charity softball league and the size and frequency of his donations to other social causes; and perhaps a relationship score based on the length of his marriage, the number of his prior divorces, instances of infidelities, and so forth.

Identifying which domains are correlated thus holds huge

value in a Reputation Economy world. And this is exactly why the next generation of reputation engines will soon eliminate the need to guess whether LeBron James would make a good babysitter; reputation scores will exist (or if they don't exist, they can be calculated) to tell you.

Portability Across Friends

If the Reputation Economy is based on making tough decisions with limited information, one of the most controversial methods will be judging you by your friends. After all, there's a lot of information in your friends' behavior: people generally (not always, but often enough) relate to similar people with similar habits and views on many issues. If there's not enough information about *you* to make a decision (extend a loan, offer a job, trust with valuable property, etc.), the reputations of your *friends* may be called in. In some ways this is the ultimate portability of reputation: not only can your own personal reputation be assessed across different domains of expertise and different contexts, but so can those of your friends.

The Framingham Heart Study, discussed in chapter 3, was just one of the first studies to find evidence of the importance of peers on your behavior. As you may recall, that study analyzed thirty years of health records and found that if one study participant gained weight, his friends and family members were likely to become more rotund as well.

It turns out that your financial fortunes are also tied to those of your friends; the more often your friends default on debt, the more likely you are to default on debt as well. A 1997 study reported that half of bankruptcy filers first found out that personal bankruptcy was an option from a friend or relative. A paper from the University of Pennsylvania revealed that the more of your friends who have declared bankruptcy, the more likely you are to do so as well—even after correcting for the fact that people tend to associate with similarly rich or poor friends.[3] A later analysis by professors from the Universities of Michigan and Chicago surmised that this could be due to the establishment of a "bankruptcy culture" that could increase the likelihood of filing by "mak[ing] households more comfortable with the idea of bankruptcy."[4] It turns out that the controversial practice of "strategic default"—simply walking away from your mortgage, leaving the bank to foreclose on your home and shoulder all the relevant expense—is also contagious. When a University of Chicago study in the midst of the housing crisis examined how strategic default (consumers often know it as "jingle mail" for the sound that house keys make when placed in an envelope addressed to the lender) spread through community networks, the study's authors found that if a home owner reported knowing a friend who had strategically defaulted, that home owner was 82 percent more likely to say that he or she also wanted to default strategically.[5]

The result of these trends among networks is that you *will* be scored on the basis of the financial prudence of your friends (at least until the practice is outlawed). If your first thought is "That's not fair," you've got a good point: most people won't default on their debts or walk away from a home mortgage, and it seems unfair to be punished just because a friend did. But if there's one theme that keeps showing up, it's that the Reputation Economy works on correlations and averages. And the stakes are high on both sides: when banks are making home mortgages for millions of dollars for thirty years at interest rates under 5 percent, very small differences in default rates can wipe out entire loan portfolios. If one group of people (borrowers with close friends who have defaulted on debt) is more risky on average than another group (borrowers with no close friends who have defaulted on debt), banks will consistently favor the less risky group—even if any given individual is unlikely to default. In short, just knowing people who are poor credit risks can make banks think that you are a worse credit risk and raise your interest rate accordingly.

Today, social media present a natural starting place for this sort of analysis. The practice of using information gleaned from social media to judge borrowers is being put to the test by a New York–based start-up originally named Movenbank (later shortened to "Moven"). Movenbank works somewhat like a traditional bank: they offer checking accounts and other financial products. But unlike traditional banks they work entirely online; they are even pushing to replace plastic credit cards with smartphone applications. And their most controversial difference from a traditional bank is their use of reputation scoring: the company has declared that it will offer accounts, credit cards, and other products on the basis of an applicant's "CREDscore." An applicant with a top CREDscore will get more exclusive offers, lower fees, and possibly even better customer service; an applicant with a low CREDscore may be denied entirely. How do they calculate these CREDscores? By accessing a customer's social networking accounts—LinkedIn, Facebook, and so on. A Movenbank proprietary algorithm then analyzes the data about you related to your job (Stable? Consistent with the income you declared?), your posting history (enough to show you're real but not so much you're skipping work to post), and your Twitter influence (extra points if you're a mover-and-shaker). Movenbank has not publicly stated that their algorithm relies on the creditworthiness of your friends, but given how easy it is to get a list of your friends from Facebook and LinkedIn, and the fact that rosters of bankruptcy filings are publicly available, it wouldn't take an MIT-level programmer to check lists of Facebook friends against public bankruptcy filings.

In other words, a machine is making important financial decisions based on your reputation *and the reputation of your friends,* without any interference from humans. If the computer thinks that your online profile looks trustworthy, you will have more access to loans and other financial products. If not, you'll be denied, possibly without explanation. This is just one of the many ways in which reputation will become portable across different situations, domains, and even individuals.

9

Inaccurate

Avoid a Social Media Oil Spill

O N JUNE 7, 2012, THOUSANDS OF INTERNET USERS were shocked by oil company Shell's new advertising campaign, which, starting with a glossy new website at ArcticReady.com, flooded the Internet with advertisements touting its progress in extracting oil from underneath frozen Arctic seas. The advertisements featured full-page high-quality stock photographs, emblazoned with messages such as "We're conquering the Arctic today to fuel a brighter tomorrow."

The ads caused an immediate uproar in social media. Twitter was immediately ablaze with complaints about Shell's tone-deaf marketing, and environmental groups and others around the Web were all but tumbling over each other to be the first to condemn Shell's insensitivity. To add fuel to the social media conflagration, Shell's site soon added a social feature that allowed visitors to easily post their own pro-drilling messages and provided easy buttons to share them with friends on Facebook and elsewhere. Thousands were quickly generated, and most were powerfully subversive. One of the most memorable user-generated images was that of an adorable Arctic fox tagged with the line "You can't run your SUV on cute" (that one got more than three hundred tweets and more than one thousand Facebook likes, in addition to thousands of untraceable shares by e-mail and on website forums).

The situation played right into the narrative of big corporations as heartless, out-of-touch, and inept with social media. The extensiveness of the campaign only made the outrage worse—not only was Shell inept, but on the basis of the number of advertisements, the size of the website, and the social media tools available, it appeared to have poured hundreds of thousands of dollars into this campaign.

There was only one problem with the popular narrative. The whole thing was a hoax. Shell had nothing to do with it at all; the environmental activist group Greenpeace had set up the fake ArcticReady.com domain, invented the fake ad campaign from whole cloth, and seeded social media with the fake advertisements. Nobody at Shell had any idea what was coming until the morning of June 7 when its PR team started receiving increasingly frantic requests for comment from reporters, each trying to get an inside scoop on the seemingly doomed advertising strategy.

In hindsight, there were some clues that the campaign was a hoax. Some of the advertisements were more than simply tone-deaf, to the point of being outright offensive: a photo of a polar bear swimming away from an oil slick with the caption "In order to survive, we all have to push our limits" is something even the most tin-eared ad agency would never publish. Even Don Draper after his drunkest three-martini lunch would have seen the problem with that ad and pulled it. But once the hoax became public it was too late. The damage had been done to Shell's reputation regardless.

Unfortunately for Shell, its troubles weren't over. Even once the hoax was revealed for what it was, many bloggers and reporters received e-mails purporting to be from Shell's PR agency and legal department, threatening that "lawyers operating on behalf of Royal Dutch Shell plc. (Shell) are considering formal action" against any websites that contributed to the spread "of potentially defamatory material on the internet." To the extent that anyone had not seen the hoax ad campaign yet, an overblown legal threat from corporate was all that was needed to make sure that every major news blog covered the story: nothing motivates bloggers more than legal threats to shut them down. Posters at top blogs from *Cryptome* to *Daily Kos* to *Boing Boing* exploded with rage at Shell's attempts to suppress coverage; it was a classic example of the "Streisand effect"[1]—a term for how any heavy-handed attempt to delete information from the Internet tends to make the information even more prominent (named after Barbra Streisand, who tried to remove photos of her house from a site showing photos of the California coastline, which led to a massive backlash and the images being posted on hundreds of sites rather than just one). The result was that bloggers became even more determined to do everything in their power to resist what seemed to be an attempt at corporate censorship of a news story.

As you might have figured out, these legal threats too were part of the hoax—the phone number for Shell's supposed legal department was routed to a fake PR firm controlled by Greenpeace in connection with its ad agency and Occupy Seattle. The e-mails themselves were sent by a Greenpeace-affiliated "culture jamming" group known as the Yes Men. The result was that even people who had not fallen for the initial ad campaign were fooled by the seemingly realistic (and all too common) overbearing response from big-law-firm lawyers.

In other words, Greenpeace's publicity campaign succeeded, perhaps beyond its creators' dreams. And even once the truth was revealed, that news never reached anything like the crescendo of outrage over Shell's advertising and subsequent legal response—as is often the case, the lies drowned out any attempts to set the record right.

And of course, thanks to the indelibility of our digital footprints, today Shell's Google results are still poisoned by the faux campaign—as of this writing, Google image searches for "Shell Arctic," "Shell drilling," "Shell safety," "Shell advertising," and many other terms still returned prominent fake advertisements, many without any indication that they were planted by Greenpeace. The "You Can't Run Your SUV on Cute" ad is still indexed by Google on at least fifty different websites. And if Twitter is any guide to popular sentiment, people are still falling for the campaign years after the fact.[2] The Greenpeace campaign is still spreading virally (if more slowly) years after its release. Even if the initial website were to be taken down today (whether voluntarily or by legal force), copies of fake advertisements have spread to tens of thousands of websites across hundreds of legal jurisdictions.

The Arctic Ready campaign was nothing short of a total brand assassination, and its success shows how powerfully and permanently inaccurate information can damage a digital reputation. Today, anyone can create lies about anyone and attribute them to somebody else: in fact, these days anyone can impersonate anyone else online—remember the "Fake Steve Jobs" who spent the years 2006 to 2011 impersonating the Steve Jobs of Apple fame?

The impact of reputation scoring systems is unmistakable. For the simple truth is that no matter how sophisticated computers and their algorithms get, they are still woefully lacking in the ability to discern fiction from fact; their ability to judge the veracity of information, in other words, has yet to catch up to the importance of the decisions they are entrusted to make.

So how can you protect yourself from such threats to your company's—or your personal—brand? The truth is that you really can't; but how you respond to that threat can either minimize or amplify the damage. When facing a total reputation assassination attempt, consider whether trying to deny or correct the false information—or even making legal threats—would make the situation better or worse. There have been successes in stopping provably false defamation by individual critics who have not yet achieved a national audience—but there have been thousands of other cases when heavy-handed defensiveness has fanned the flames rather than smothering them. Once the fake response from Shell was produced, the images of the fake campaign had already spread to thousands of websites and would be effectively impossible to remove.

Of course, few people will be on the receiving end of an attack as elaborate or damaging as the one on Shell, but consider the more everyday reputation threats faced by hundreds of small businesses. For instance, competitors leaving fake negative Yelp reviews or paying people to post negative comments from fake users and so on can slowly destroy a business's reputation, one fake comment at a time. So how to respond?

Choose Direct or Indirect Action

First, if something negative does appear in your search results or digital résumé, you need to decide whether you will take direct or indirect action. Just as the best boxers sometimes value their dodge and weave as much as their striking ability, you can learn to slip out from attacks without direct confrontation.

It could take an entire book to explain the rules for responding to reputation assassination, but here's a condensed version. First, if you are accused of something that is false and you can *objectively* and *unequivocally* prove it false, consider a public response directly refuting the allegation. The danger with any direct response, of course, as we learned from the example above, is that you draw more attention to the conflict and you may come across as aggressive or defensive. So the basic rule of thumb is to consider how a neutral third party would feel if he or she read your response: you will probably never convince a malicious detractor anyway, but it may be worth your while if you can help set the record straight for third parties. But unless you are absolutely certain that a third party would see you as the rational, calm party, then don't respond directly.

If you do choose to respond directly, set the record straight as widely as you can *without drawing undue attention to the original allegation.* If, for example, you are accused in a blog post of having been fired when you actually resigned voluntarily, you may be able to prove that allegation false with photos of your going-away party, a copy of a letter you received from the department head saying you were a great employee, or even just your positive LinkedIn reviews from the job. Make sure these items are posted in places at least as prominent as the attack: your personal blog, Twitter, LinkedIn, and so on. You may not need to even mention that you were ever attacked, but make it unmistakable to a neutral reader that you have nothing to hide.

Sometimes additional context is necessary to refute a false story. When that happens, follow the lead of the game company OnLive and help provide that context. When the small game publisher OnLive was experiencing some business difficulties, rather than filing for bankruptcy, management worked out a deal to sell most of the working assets to a new company that would continue the OnLive name and continue to employ most of the company's staff. The problem arose because the transaction meant that all of the staff lost any stock options they had in the "old" OnLive. The game development community is close-knit and is very sensitive to any sense that developers are being taken advantage of. So when word got out that developers' options were being wiped out, an angry gaming community lashed out at the company for seemingly taking advantage of its hardworking staff. But, over the days and weeks that followed, company supporters and executives carefully explained that any value in the stock options had already been destroyed by the narrowly avoided bankruptcy and that by selling off the company's assets the company was able to at least preserve developer jobs. Not all developers ultimately accepted the company's line, but the additional context did help rehabilitate OnLive's reputation, and the company was able soon to resume recruitment.

Sometimes, though, even when there is more story to tell, setting the record straight is futile and the best thing to do is to simply move on—as in the case of the campaign that was launched around the question "Why is Progressive Insurance morally bankrupt?" when the company forced a grieving family to jump through legal hoops to recover uninsured motorist coverage after their daughter was killed in a car crash by an uninsured driver. When faced with a brand attack like that, there's not a lot a company can do; after all, nearly any answer to that question would just make the situation worse. Progressive (correctly but perhaps unwisely) pointed out that the procedure it followed was legally correct and was the standard practice in the industry, but the more it protested, the more it drew attention to the story. Ultimately, it was trying to fight an emotion-based argument with reason, and that rarely works.

Progressive's best answer was ultimately to walk away, quietly pay off the family, and stop trying to defend its conduct. There was no factual rebuttal it could give to the emotion-laden argument of seemingly not paying a grieving family. If you ever find yourself in a similar situation, it's best to just move the discussion to other areas of the business instead of drawing more attention by trying to downplay the controversy.

Be Alert

As we've seen, hits to your digital reputation will be instant, whether they are based on fact or fiction. Like hurricanes in September, online rumors can start quietly and quickly spin up into a full-blown storm within days (or even hours). But if you stay alert, you can steer the storm away—or at least take shelter and board up the windows.

For example, take the Kony 2012 campaign. As many will recall, this began when the movement to bring African warlord Joseph Kony to justice went viral on Facebook, seemingly overnight. Within days, nearly everyone was talking about how positive the Kony 2012 campaign was (and how reprehensible Mr. Kony himself was). But, just as quickly, the tide began to turn against the Kony 2012 campaign and its founder Jason Russell. Discussions of racism, perceptions of Africa, and other topics began to undermine the campaign, and Russell soon became the unintentional center of attention when he suffered a meltdown standing naked as a jaybird on a street corner in San Diego and yelling at cars. The story became about him rather than the (very real) human rights abuses in Africa. But because the organization stayed alert and vigilant, it was able to recognize the growing storm and launch a new flood of content about Kony that put the focus back where it should be—on the serious issue of warlordism in Africa, rather than on the silly indiscretions of the movement's founder.

Large companies are often slower to spot the signs of a gathering storm. For example, Apple fairly recently faced a (false) rumor that it had built its newest generation of products using screws that were incompatible with all currently existing screwdrivers, in a deliberate attempt to make it impossible for anyone other than its own repair technicians to fix its products. The story turned out to be a complete hoax,[3] but it created a massive social media uproar before Apple was able to quell the rumors. Had Apple spotted the storm brewing earlier, it could have interceded and spread the truth before the hoax went viral and worldwide.

Individual Brand Assassination

It's not just businesses that are subject to the danger of reputation assassination, of course; individuals are at risk as well. Examples of our personal and professional reputations being compromised by false or misleading online information are all too common already (and in many ways are more difficult to uncover because most individuals don't have legal departments and PR teams to call upon when attacked). Further, misinformation and mischaracterizations can be just as harmful as some attacks.

In fact, despite the technological sophistication of many Reputation Economy methods of scoring individuals, they are still highly prone to error. For example, online programming code repository GitHub.com enjoyed a brief moment in the sun as a supposed hot spot for tech firms looking to find top developers—and as a supposed replacement for traditional résumés. The theory went that instead of submitting a résumé based on job experience, programmers would simply direct potential employers to view all of the code they had written and stored on GitHub.

But if you're a programmer, don't throw away that heavy cotton résumé paper yet. GitHub has not yet revolutionized the world of hiring. For one, it shows only contributions to projects that are public and have online code repositories. Most work done for private employers isn't publicly available, and even very productive developers working on the free and open-source Chrome operating system don't show up in GitHub because the Chrome project uses a different code repository. And forget trying to showcase your competency at any activities other than just writing code; GitHub doesn't give any credit for activities like crafting product strategy or mentoring junior developers, let alone forms of expression like film, writing, management, sales, R&D, and customer service. The result is a particularly pernicious form of inaccuracy: false precision that makes it seem as if people are being fairly scored when they really are scored on only a tiny subset of their work.

Social scoring systems like Klout (increasingly being used by HR departments for hiring and other decision making) can also be woefully inaccurate: consider that Warren Buffett initially got a Klout score of only 36/100.[4] Known as the "Sage of Omaha," Buffett holds an annual investor conference that attracts thirty thousand visitors, who caravan from around the country to pay upwards of $250 per ticket to attend an event treated as the Super Bowl of investing,[5] and his annual newsletters are read by millions of retail investors and by nearly every investment professional. Along similar lines, consider Buffett's role in the success of Berkshire Hathaway, where a single share of stock that cost around $20.50 at the end of 1967 would have increased in value to more than $178,000 by early 2013. Even during the 2000–2010 decade, which was widely disastrous for stocks (even the S&P 500 returned negative 11.3 percent), Berkshire Hathaway stock increased 76 percent. But if you made investing decisions on the basis of Klout scores you'd pass right by Buffett. His score was lower than that of aspiring journalist Lesley Hauler, for example (if you haven't heard of her, don't worry: most people other than her 631 Twitter followers[6] haven't, despite her Klout score of 60/100).[7] In fairness, Klout has updated its algorithm in light of the obvious disparity between Buffett's influence and his score—as of this writing he scores in the 80s—but the fact that he was scored below 50 for so long demonstrates how Klout's estimate of people's influence can be completely inaccurate.

Another criticism of Klout—perhaps due more to its popularity than to its being more problematic than any other similar service—is that its rankings can be subject to powerful manipulation. For example, a digital marketing manager named Adriaan Pelzer was able to use "bots" (automated messages written by automated programs) to generate Klout scores up to 51/100—a very high score relative to most real humans.[8] And when a guy named Neil Kodner went even further and created bots that automatically responded to tweets about celebrities like Seinfeld and Sarah Palin—each bot simply tweeted a randomly selected quote about that celebrity—his "@HelloooooNewman" Twitter account accumulated a Klout score of 74/100—twice that of Warren Buffett—for a while.[9]

Some Source Data Is Outright Wrong

The expression "Garbage in, garbage out" refers to the fact that even the most sophisticated computer will produce inaccurate information as output if the only input data it has to work with is inaccurate. So the big danger online is that a reputation scoring system will produce what appears to be good and useful data even if it is actually steer manure. After all, it's easy to believe a score that comes from a complex proprietary algorithm and appears to be based on hundreds of sources. But if the underlying data is garbage (and it probably is), the output will be too.

How commonly do reputation engines get fed bad input data? To answer this question, consider that the largest public company in the world (at least for much of 2012–13) is actively pursuing patents on ways to mislead online data aggregators. Indeed, Apple has already received one patent on a system that misconstrues your online identity by creating automated network activity that is similar (but not identical) to yours. So if you search Google for "vacations in Spain," Apple's patented system might, for example, automatically search Google for "vacations in Italy" and "vacations in Portugal" as well. Of course, this seems pretty harmless when all you are doing is searching vacation destinations, but imagine the inferences that will be drawn if you appear to be searching for jobs at five different companies instead of just one (your current employer, in looking at your search history, would think you were searching for a new job instead of perhaps researching just one for a work-related purpose, or helping a friend), or five different searches on ways to dispose of a body instead of just one (it would look as if you were plotting a murder versus fact-checking your favorite police TV show) or any of a hundred other wrong assumptions.

Even if you aren't an Apple user, don't get too comfortable, because there's a free and open-source program that does the same. The program TrackMeNot is published at a ".nyu.edu" address and is promoted as a privacy enhancer.[10] When enabled, it runs automatic Google searches for random terms so that Google has a more difficult time identifying individual users. Depending on a user's goals, it is even possible to ask it to flood your search history with terms to throw anyone who might be monitoring your searches—like the government—off the scent; after all, if you search for hundreds or even thousands of random terms per day, it will be much harder for the government to identify any "real" searches you're running.[11]

And some Web publishers are trying to trick Google and other search engines by "mashing up" different Web pages at random, in the hope that Google will think that the result is real content and send search visitors to these mashed-up pages, thus earning the publisher advertising revenue for each visitor who lands on one of these pages. It is a meager game—publishers of this form of Web spam create hundreds of millions of pages in the hopes of gaining tenths of a cent in views per page—but it is also extremely cheap to play; one computer robot ("bot") simply jumps from link to link across the Internet scraping Web pages, and another bot randomly combines them into new pages. The result is that if your name has been mentioned in any kind of prominent directory or news site, it has probably also been mashed up into Web spam somewhere.

Usually this is harmless enough, but occasionally it can be directly dangerous to your reputation. For example, imagine what could happen if one of these random Web-scraping bots mashed up a page listing civic activists with a list of Megan's Law sex offenders to create a new page that Google would index. The bot wouldn't intend to sow confusion; it would just be randomly mixing pages together. But the result would be that your name would become associated with sex offenders, completely erroneously. For another example, author Michael Fertik's name is plastered in a random compilation of posts in what appears to be a spam blog trying to sell advertisements for phones and cameras—hardly a direct threat to his reputation, but enough to possibly confuse the reputation engine of a potential employer, investor, or anyone else looking for information about his career and areas of expertise.[12]

Luckily, unlike other false information that probably exists about you around the Web, this one is fairly easy to detect; if you Google your name and see a notice that "some duplicate results have been hidden," just click the button to see the extra results and find out how your name is being used in this sort of digital babble. Unfortunately, if you do find that your name has been mashed up in some undesirable way, there isn't a lot you can do about it, since the system is automated and you'll probably never be able to track down the original publisher anyway. But simply being aware of it so that you can be prepared to explain it if it comes up on a job interview or a date will help minimize the damage.

Each of these errors probably has a small impact individually, but they are representative of the larger prevalence of intentionally scrambled data being created and published online. And just as fast as erroneous, mixed-up data can be cataloged, more can be created, setting in motion the vicious feedback loop we talked about earlier in the chapter. Remember, automated reputation scoring systems that rely on digital data—in other words, just about all of them—can easily be fooled by this flood of digital debris, and the more of this digital flotsam washes into reputation engines, the harder it is for even the most responsible and sophisticated reputation engines to sort out the truth.

Looking for Love in (What a Computer Thinks Are) All the Right Places

Despite all of the inaccuracies in your digital footprint, make no mistake that your digital reputation is still being used to make incredibly intimate decisions about your future. Take, for example, your romantic prospects. These days, online dating is big business. The size of the market is huge. In 2011, leading site Match.com bought for $50 million a small competitor called OKCupid.com, which attracted more than 1.3 million unique visitors per month. Free dating site PlentyOfFish boasts more than 6 billion (yes, 6,000,000,000) page views per month, and its value is estimated to be in the range of $200 million to $1 billion. More niche sites—like FarmersOnly and Trek Passions (yes, for Trekkies)—are cropping up every day.

But online dating, in the early days especially, has been particularly flawed. Online dating was supposed to solve the problems of meeting people in bars; bars are loud and crowded, interactions are often shallow, meeting new people can be dangerous (particularly for women), and there is an excess of antisocial behavior (particularly by men). But early online dating merely replicated the problems of bars: sites were designed to allow users to quickly skim hundreds of photos of potential mates (shallow), and personal questions were often inane (it turns out that few people dislike sushi, puppies, or "most kinds of music.") Plus the sites' algorithms did nothing to screen unsavory users, and women often complained about barrages of offensive messages from men. In effect, these first-generation dating sites just moved a bar into the convenience of a user's living room. But in the new second or third wave of online dating, a new range of flaws is emerging: inaccuracy due to poor computer modeling and data collection.

One second-generation site called eHarmony tried to replace the meat market with something closer to a traditional, *Fiddler on the Roof*–style matchmaking system. Psychologist and marriage counselor Neil Clark Warren thought that he could identify the shared traits that most often led to successful relationships and could build a model that would evaluate each new user and then pair couples on the basis of these traits. The problem is that the site's only basis to match users is a 258-question survey that each new user must complete, meaning that the survey is subject to all the normal problems of bias introduced by self-reporting. (Separately, the site also ran into difficulty when it was sued in several states for matching only heterosexual couples but refusing to match same-sex couples; the company has since launched a site called Compatible Partners to address the disparity.)

eHarmony isn't alone; the entire current generation of dating sites rely almost entirely on self-reporting about personality traits: Do you prefer rock or rap? Want children or none? Prefer art or the outdoors? But this system utterly fails to identify many traits that are very important to potential mates. For example, there is no good way to find out if users are polite and respectful. Asking directly will lead to predictably skewed answers, if not outright lies. Even asking more behaviorally based questions—such as whether users are consistently on time—will lead to similar skewing. Further (as many daters find out too late), asking if a user is already in another relationship, or even married, will not always elicit a truthful response. Asking "Are you honest?" creates a logical inconsistency that would melt even Spock's brain.

In an attempt to reduce the inaccuracies resulting from self-reporting, a dating start-up called Yoke (perhaps doomed by its name) briefly tried to use a more advanced version of reputation scoring. It forced users to log in using Facebook and then judged their "real" personality on the basis of activities such as their "likes" on Facebook, products reviewed on Amazon.com, and movies rated on Netflix. It even made judgments about people on the basis of where they went to college (while the details of college matching were fuzzy, one can assume that the system would discount matches between alumni of schools such as Smith and Brigham Young). From these data points, the system calculated similarity scores and tried to match users with common interests. For example, a user who rated *Arrested Development* highly on Netflix would be matched with a user who bought a box set of *The Office* on Amazon.[13] The system fizzled, however, as users became concerned about the privacy implications of using Facebook for dating; users were (perhaps justifiably) concerned that their Facebook friends would learn about their dating profiles, dates would e-stalk them, and Facebook would use their data in unexpected ways. In other words, Yoke captured all the downsides of reputation networks (privacy concerns) without effectively capturing the beneficial parts (networks of trust and reputation through peers). In a way, it ended up perhaps more creepy than effective—there are so many ways that people misrepresent themselves (consciously and not) in their Facebook profiles that the data ended up being terrible anyway.

There are already signs that dating start-ups are taking the next step of capturing the valuable parts of reputation networks. A site by the name of TheComplete.me (again, naming seems to be a difficulty for creators of such sites), for example, matches by many of the same characteristics as Yoke (shared interests) but also by your social network: Who are your most frequent chat partners, whose posts do you like, and with whom do you interact?[14] And others are trying to minimize the creepy factor. For example, "Circl.es" (yet more challenging naming) also heavily relies on Facebook data; it launched with a "meat market" interface based on user photos, but it improves on Yoke by guaranteeing more privacy.

It is all but certain that future sites will also use your reputation *within* your social network (What are your friends saying about you?) and the reputation *of* your social network (What are people saying about your friends?) to evaluate whether a suitor really is courteous, prompt, honest . . . *and* actually single. They can do this by searching for what other people, ranging from friends to exes to public records, have said about you (whether on Facebook, Twitter, or the open Internet), then aggregating and analyzing that data to assign you a score for each relevant trait. But by capturing how other people see you rather than relying on self-reporting, these algorithms will be able not only to weed out deceptions and mischaracterizations but also to more accurately predict which potential partners you will be most compatible with—thus serving up more matches who are more apt to like you, and whom you are more apt to like.

In some ways, this is no different from the service provided by high-end matchmakers, who interview friends and family to get an unbiased (or at least less biased) view of their clients and do background checks on the people they set up with their clients. Or, as we've seen, in some ways it's a return to small town reputation, where a local matchmaker (think Yenta from *Fiddler on the Roof*) knows the truth about everyone in the town, for better or worse, and incorporates years of practice (and experience from watching the results) into pairing up couples.

If you're the sort of person who gets rave reviews from friends (and maybe even warm reviews from exes), congratulations—you'll be rewarded and have plentiful high-quality dating choices while all the sleazy individuals have their dirty laundry aired. If not, well, it's not too soon to start burnishing your image. Reconcile with anyone who is publicly complaining about you (to the extent possible, of course) and clean up all the photos of you pounding tequila shots on spring break (or whatever your vice is). Use better grammar and diction in your public profile—you don't have to be perfect, but be good enough to not stand out for poor grammar. Remove outdated information, like an old MySpace profile that says "in a relationship" simply because you haven't updated it in years.

And remember to temper your expectations: any website that tries to predict matters of the heart with an algorithm, however sophisticated, is not likely to have a huge success rate. Computer screening will never fully replace human interaction in dating: people will always find each other interesting and attractive in ways that computers could never replicate (and for a while yet, it seems likely that humans will still decide for themselves which prospects they would like to meet in person). But like DAMM in job searching, computerized reputation will still have a powerful filtering effect. If the computer algorithm assumes you would be a poor fit with certain potential partners, you'll probably never know that those people exist in the first place; you'll never see their profile, they'll never see yours, and you'll never know why. And it can all be thrown off by a simple input error, something as little as mistaking your reference to the song "Hold On" to mean the Jonas Brothers song (and making corresponding judgments about your taste in music) when you really meant the version by Kansas (or Korn or Tom Waits or any of several other completely different songs by that name).

Finally, stay alert. You don't need another reminder about how fast online rumors can spread and how the Internet can drag things out of context—you already know. What you need is awareness. Google Alerts are one easy, free way to stay on top of changes to your search results. Set them up for your name, your name plus your profession, your name plus your employer/department, and anything else you think might be relevant. Through careful monitoring and taking action (when appropriate), you can help prevent inaccuracies from spreading. Knowledge is power—on the Web and elsewhere.

10

Proactive

Own the Conversation

JUST BECAUSE YOUR REPUTATION IN THE REPUTATION Economy has hit a snag doesn't mean you need to give up. In this way your digital reputation is more like a stock portfolio than a bank account; it may swing between highs and lows, and even if you dip way down into the red, you can always bounce back to black. The key is to be proactive; if you can control what people are measuring—and what people are talking about—you can change the conversation in your favor.

Take an example from before the Reputation Economy kicked off full-force. In the 1990s, automaker Hyundai's reputation was in the pits. The Korean manufacturer had first tried to enter the U.S. market in 1986 with the Hyundai Excel. The compact car started strong, setting a record for first-year import sales in the United States by selling more than 168,000 cars in that first year. The car's competitive advantage was low price.

At a sticker price of a mere $4,995 it handily beat most Detroit makes—it was literally half the price of a Ford Taurus, or about the same price as only eighty-three of 1986's breakout Teddy Ruxpin toy bears.[1] But soon after launch, the car began to earn a reputation for being not only inexpensive but also (perhaps not surprisingly) cheaply made: the seats frayed quickly, and reports of badly rusted underbodies and jammed window cranks began to emerge.[2] By the 1990s, fewer than one hundred thousand were being sold each year, and Hyundai franchisees began to walk away from the automaker.

To add insult to injury, the brand became a cinematic punch line: 1992's boiler room sales drama *Glengarry Glen Ross* featured sales trainer Alec Baldwin putting a less skilled salesman in his place by reminding him that "you drove a Hyundai to get here tonight, I drove an $80,000 BMW" (just in case the point wasn't clear, he later reiterated that "[my] watch cost more than your car").[3] Even Jay Leno cracked that it was easy for Hyundai owners to double the value of their car: just fill the tank with gas.

Through the 1990s, Hyundai sales remained mired under one hundred thousand units per year. It didn't help that the 1990s were a cruel decade for small carmakers; the 1990s saw the demise of both Geo and Eagle, and Chrysler was also struggling, with fewer than fifty thousand sales annually under its own nameplate (and shortly thereafter merged with Daimler-Benz in a transaction that many believed to be a buyout by the larger German maker).[4] Even Plymouth, averaging around 140,000 cars per year in the late 1990s, was scrapped by 2001.[5] Hyundai's low sales and diminishing footprint had made the manufacturer so deeply irrelevant that the automotive business press was no longer even reporting on Hyundai, entirely omitting it from many monthly sales reports.[6] The writing was on the wall: unless Hyundai turned around its reputation, it would be forced to exit the lucrative U.S. market, possibly forever.

Facing this very real threat as sales continued to slump and franchise losses became self-perpetuating, Hyundai took bold action. Its leaders knew that its cars could meet the standards of the American brands—it analyzed its own warranty claims and saw a marked improvement in quality from its initial U.S. launch.[7] But executives also knew that the make's reputation for low quality would not be easy to rehabilitate. Instead of attacking perceptions directly, Hyundai did one better: the company got proactive and changed the discussion entirely. In 1998, the company made headlines by rewriting the book on warranty coverage, offering buyers a then unheard-of "10-year, 100,000-mile" power train warranty across its entire lineup, and launching a multimillion-dollar national ad campaign promoting what it called a "decade of durability" on every new car sold.

Today, some other automakers have caught up in their coverage—or at least met partway—but at the time the idea of a ten-year power train warranty was bewildering compared to the industry standard of three years. For a brand of cars perceived as cheap and failure-prone, the offer seemed even more shocking: How could Hyundai possibly support a ten-year no-deductible, no-cost extended warranty given its history of manufacturing defects? Hyundai U.S. CEO John Krafcik called it a "bet-the-company move," and indeed it was.[8]

The result was that suddenly Hyundai was back in the news, for better or for worse.[9] Car review publisher Edmunds listed the details of the warranty and instructed its subscribers to "read that again, and be impressed" before calling the warranty "a perfect plan for erasing any lingering concerns about Hyundai's reliability."[10] Others called it "one of the industry's most comprehensive consumer warranty programs."[11] Even local papers like the *Reading Eagle* of Berks County, Pennsylvania (automotive section cover story: "Local Limousine Drivers Reveal Their Secrets for Getting to Philadelphia, New York on Time") covered the warranty story, sparking a new narrative about Hyundai.[12] Importantly, none focused on the question of quality improvement itself, which would have just reinforced the subconscious perception of Hyundai as a low-quality make. Instead, all spent most of their ink comparing Hyundai's warranty to that of other import and domestic makes—and that comparison at the time was purely positive for Hyundai.

The gambit worked: in 1999, Hyundai sold 82 percent more cars than in the prior year. By 2006, Hyundai was selling more than 450,000 cars annually, representing 2.8 percent of the U.S. auto market. By 2010, that figure had leapt again, to more than 530,000 cars for 4.6 percent of the U.S. market.[13] In 2012, Hyundai sold over 700,000 cars in the United States under its badge—surpassing longtime players such as Dodge, Jeep, and Volkswagen. In fact, Hyundai in 2012 went so far as to beat traditional luxury makes BMW, Mercedes, and Infiniti—*combined*.[14]

Of course, a new warranty by itself didn't rescue Hyundai; management made plenty of other smart decisions on topics ranging from quality control through design through pricing. But the very public discussion of the new warranty was necessary to repair the brand's reputation for low quality by changing the conversation in a positive way. Instead of talking about quality, consumers started talking about warranty coverage; say what you would about the car's shoddy seats and window cranks, you couldn't argue that Hyundai wasn't the far and away leader in warranty coverage. Hyundai, in other words, successfully shifted the discussion from its greatest weakness to its biggest strength.

As we've seen throughout this book, in the Reputation Economy all of your strengths and weaknesses will be cataloged, permanently, like it or not. But while you can't control what information is or isn't recorded about you, you can, at least to some extent, control to what information—positive or negative—people's focus is drawn. This chapter is about how.

Be Shocking

Hyundai's "Best American Warranty" campaign demonstrates another important lesson about challenging an existing narrative: the need to be shocking to break up existing mind-sets. Hyundai didn't just somewhat improve its warranty; it did something shocking by tripling its own warranty and more than doubling that of the nearest competitor. That made it not just a good warranty but a warranty that people talked about. In an era when many imports weren't expected to run much past one hundred thousand miles, Hyundai shocked the public by offering something that seemed almost too good to be true.

The concept of shaking up a bad reputation with something shocking enough to make headlines, of course, works in other realms as well. In fact, in every area of the Reputation Economy, one highly visible and publicized move can often generate enough press to effectively drown out older messages. In fact, even with great algorithms, reputation engines are subject to the same bias as humans in that they are apt to pay too much attention to newsworthy events. Even when there's not a lot of data to collect and analyze about them, they are disproportionately weighted nonetheless.

Consider how some stale technology companies have taken advantage of this in attempts to revamp their reputations. After its prominence in the 1990s, Yahoo!'s brand slowly deteriorated through the first part of the 2000s. The Yahoo! Directory had long been surpassed by Google search, and Yahoo! no longer even maintained its own search engine (its search results were powered by Microsoft's Bing engine). Yahoo!'s e-mail products failed to keep up with Google's Gmail, and it lacked a hardware product like the one Microsoft had in the Xbox. By the early-mid 2010s, Yahoo! faced a serious reputation challenge: it was seen as outdated, slow-moving, and no longer on the cutting edge. If the company didn't change something soon, it would enter a downward spiral in which its reputation would seriously blunt its recruiting ability, which would hurt its ability to create new products, further blunting its reputation . . . you get the idea.

So in 2012, Yahoo! surprised everyone in the industry (including some of the company's own top executives) with an unexpected and splashy new hire, bucking all the industry expectations by passing over everyone on the expected CEO short list to instead hire then Google executive Marissa Mayer. But if the media coverage of Mayer's hire gave the company's reputation a temporary boost, the company's reputational troubles reemerged full-force once Mayer set about trying to make Yahoo! relevant again. Many of her initial moves were met with widespread hostility, most notably her decision to abruptly change the company's telecommuting policy. Although the change affected only a few employees, this was viewed as a symbolic move, prompting reporters and bloggers all over the country to question whether Mayer was going to enforce a new culture of rigidity that would further alienate Yahoo!'s already beleaguered workforce. In a bit of unfortunate timing, the week after the telecommuting memo was publicized, it also became public that Mayer had installed a nursery in an adjoining office so that she could visit her child during the day. As the *New York Daily News* headline put it, "Yahoo! honcha Marissa Mayer outrages minions by building nursery near her office after barring employees from working from home."[15]

After the two negative stories in a row about Yahoo!'s internal policies, Mayer needed to do something big to focus attention elsewhere. For so long as the media spent its ink on the company's internal issues, Mayer would be unable to effect the changes needed to rescue Yahoo!

An opportunity soon came in the form of the popular microblogging site Tumblr. At the time, Tumblr was the hottest social media property on the market, in stark comparison to the tumbleweed (no pun intended) that characterized Yahoo!'s meager social offerings at the time (some gaming sites and the no longer trendy photo-sharing site Flickr). So Mayer decided to go big or go home, paying a staggering $1 billion for Tumblr, acquiring a massive user base and also a new direction for the future.

Reaction in the media and across the blogosphere was instant. The business press had been looking for a story of Yahoo!'s resurgence or failure; Mayer's bold decision gave them a story to run with. One analyst called it the move that "put the yippee back into Yahoo" and made the company "relevant once again in Silicon Valley."[16]

Giving people a bold headline to focus on allowed Mayer and Yahoo! to change the discussion to a territory favorable to them. But you don't have to be CEO of a major technology company to employ such a tactic. Any big move that changes people's expectations of you can change how you're being measured. Tired of being "that guy" who is known around the office for being the go-to for drinking on Friday night? Make a big and visible commitment to a charity event or a team-in-training instead. Tired of being known for eating poorly? Join a CrossFit gym and bombard your coworkers with CrossFit photos. In each case, it's a response that runs perpendicular to the information you're trying to overcome—not trying to defend yourself, simply changing the conversation.

Frame the Debate Before It Can Even Start

When Facebook built a massive energy-consuming data center in Prineville, Oregon, it provided a great lesson in framing the debate *before the debate even happens.* You may not realize that every time you visit the website Facebook.com, your computer sends a request to a data center somewhere far away. That data center pulls together a variety of information—your friends' activities, photos, news updates, and more—and sends it instantaneously back to you. When Facebook started, these operations were all controlled by one computer running in Mark Zuckerberg's dorm room. Today, it takes tens of thousands of computers to manage these operations for hundreds of thousands of simultaneous users, and these computers are housed in massive data centers.

By necessity, these tens of thousands of computers consume huge amounts of electricity to run: even without screens attached, each server may draw nearly 500 watts. In 2013, Facebook was estimated to run more than sixty thousand servers, which soon raised a rather important question: Where to keep them?[17]

Facebook recognized that the high desert of Oregon would be an ideal place for a data center: cool temperatures would minimize cooling costs, and plentiful electricity would power its computers. But when Facebook started building the first phase of its data center in Prineville, Oregon, it realized that it would be facing an image challenge. Oregon has long been a heart of the environmental movement (remember the spotted owl controversy of the 1990s, when Oregon environmentalists and loggers went head to head over habitat for an owl species?), and data centers are massive power users: the first phase of the Prineville project alone is zoned to draw up to 15 megawatts of power—more than the entire consumption of the island nation of Togo.[18] In the era of climate change and carbon awareness, building a data center in Oregon seemed a publicity disaster waiting to happen.

So Facebook decided to be proactive and frame the conversation *before* it happened. Instead of focusing on the total energy consumed by the facility (literally larger than some countries'), Facebook's PR team cherry-picked a measurement that would be favorable to it—how efficiently that energy was being used—and repeatedly publicized its measurement of its own "power usage effectiveness" (simply a measurement of what proportion of data center energy is actually being used by computers). It is a particularly creative measurement because it distracts from the total power consumption (massive) and makes it seem as though Facebook is being efficient, thus allowing Facebook to entirely dodge the questions of how many computers are actually required, how far data must travel that it otherwise wouldn't, and what environmental ramifications that has. Yet journalists and others, being pressed by rolling deadlines, accepted it.

To complete the narrative, Facebook created "rare" press tours, again focusing on the power efficiency of the facility.[19] Visiting reporters drove past a small solar installation (that "doesn't provide much power for the system") and were shown live measurements of the "power usage effectiveness" on a display.[20] Of course, the monitor showing the power usage was complete with a background image of a beautiful Oregon lake, at least subconsciously associating the center with ecology and nature.

Like Hyundai and Yahoo!, Facebook made sure to include at least one stunning fact: the center has no air conditioner. Most data centers feature large commercial air conditioners on the roof, using traditional Freon-type coolant to keep computers at room temperature. Instead, Facebook's data center uses a mist system to cool ambient air flowing through the data center—much like a swamp chiller. The system worked great until unexpected conditions caused a cloud to form inside the three-story structure, raining water and short-circuiting several computers.[21] Yet somewhat incredibly, what could have been a PR disaster turned out to actually be a boost to Facebook's reputation: the story of an actual cloud inside Facebook's "cloud" computing center only served to reinforce Facebook's narrative of the data center as ecologically efficient.

By focusing attention on a metric on which Facebook knew itself to excel—the whole data center was designed to optimize the "power usage effectiveness"—it was able to focus much of the press attention on that metric rather than the hundreds of other metrics on which it might not excel. It just goes to show that even if all of those other data points are being collected and analyzed in the Reputation Economy, they can't hurt you if nobody is looking at them.

Hustle, Don't Get Hustled

These techniques of focusing attention on your strengths—and even creating new measurements of those strengths if existing ones don't work—are just as applicable to individuals as to corporations.

Consider the old bar advice to "never bet on the other man's game." In addition to being good advice to avoid getting hustled on bar bets, it's savvy advice for reputation management in the Reputation Economy. The original principle is simple: if a stranger walks up to you in a bar and offers a friendly wager on a game of pool, you'd be a fool to accept. Even if you're reasonably handy around a cue, there is a pretty good chance this stranger has chosen to bet on pool for a reason—he's a hustler or a shark. This advice is hardly new; turn-of-the-twentieth-century actor William A. Brady may have been the first to commit it to the pages of the *New York Times* when, in 1901, he described an incident in which he was hustled by a man who, of all things, could measure unfamiliar objects with uncanny accuracy (it turned out the stranger simply had memorized a list of known lengths—the distance from his elbow to each finger, from his knee to shin, the length of his foot, etc.) and paid a price for his education.[22] Brady's parting advice, "Never bet when the other fellow makes the proposition," holds equally in today's Reputation Economy.

The application to your individual reputation is twofold. First, don't let somebody else choose how they're being compared to you. If you and another division manager are competing for a promotion, be wary if your competitor is trying to draw attention to revenue growth per division: he's probably carefully selected that metric for a reason. Don't let him control the basis for comparison.

Second, if you can control the subject of conversation, you can make sure it is playing to your strength. Just as the barroom stranger wants to play pool (or place bets on the size of objects) because those are his strengths, you can profit from playing to yours. Hyundai moved the conversation from reliability to its warranty. Yahoo! moved the conversation away from the staleness of their innovation to their new celebrity CEO and their billion-dollar acquisitions. Instead of trying to compete on quality or "hipness"—both losing propositions—Hyundai and Yahoo played the games they knew they could win.

There is almost certainly *something* at which you excel. If you're a business and you've been around for more than a few years, it's very likely that you are excelling in at least one area. Take, for example, Costco and Walmart. There is little doubt that Walmart has an unassailable reputation as the low-price leader for everyday purchases—its supply chain efficiency is studied in business curricula worldwide. But Costco has successfully held its own against its lower-priced competitor by refusing to bet on the other man's game. When confronted by head-on competition with Walmart, Costco is quick to emphasize that its workers are paid better (an average of $17 per hour, compared to $10 at Walmart) and receive better benefits.[23] High-wage employees aren't a direct benefit to customers, but it doesn't matter. Costco is trying to do exactly what we've been taking about in this chapter: move the conversation away from pricing to *values*— promoting a living wage and building a stronger community.

Prices and wages are hardly the only options available to you in deciding what area of excellence you want to flaunt about your business. Businesses might frame the conversation around cheap versus healthy food, biggest selection versus locally owned, and countless other topics. Your company of business's record on all of these dimensions can be scored and measured—and it will—but remember, ultimately a human will have to decide which is more important (low prices or a living wage, cheap or healthy, selection versus community), and the smart businesses are the ones who frame the conversation to tip the scales of that decision in their favor.

As an individual, you can do the same simply by calling out attention to aspects of your reputation that no one can beat. Have you been named employee of the month four times in a row? Have you grossed the top sales in your department for two years straight? Have you had a perfect credit score since the day you turned eighteen? These are probably achievements no one can argue or compete with. Tout them, as loudly as you can.

For in a world where people are going to be talking about you no matter what, the best thing you can do is ensure that *you* control the conversation, frame the issues, and paint yourself in the best light possible.

Be an Innovator

IF THERE'S ONE THING CERTAIN ABOUT THE REPUTATION Economy, it is that with it come opportunities for innovators and early adopters like you to gain an advantage—to gain a world-class reputation while others remain stuck in the hall of shame or, worse, buried in the fine print of the phone book for decades. But the fruits of the Reputation Economy are as sweet for individual consumers as they are for entrepreneurs and businesses. Consider that ten years ago it would have been impossible to travel to a strange city and within hours of landing rent out a huge room in a stranger's apartment in the ideal location, rent another stranger's car for an hour for a fraction of the going rate, and or even have dinner with yet a third stranger at a local, underground hot spot not listed in any travel guide. But thanks to services like Airbnb, Wheelz, and GrubWithUs, all these are possible. Each service depends on reputation to work, and each enables new transactions—benefiting both the entrepreneur and the consumer—that would have been impossible before the Reputation Economy.

For example, take Couchsurfing.org, which matches travelers with people willing to take on free visitors. In the couchsurfing model, strangers meet and exchange a night's stay for a good story, a yodeling lesson, a bottle of wine, or whatever else the guest can provide. Lest this sound like some hippie counterculture diversion, let me assure you that the site claims more than 6 million users (although this may include some nonactive or retired profiles). The point is that this service is powered entirely by reputation—without reputation to serve as a filter, the dangers of opening one's home to strangers (or visiting someone else's) are far too great, whether the exchange is paid for in yodeling lessons or dollars. Couchsurfing.org approached the trust problem as a network: the site's founders designated certain of their friends as trustworthy, who in turn were able to designate others as trustworthy, who in turn designated more as trusted. The result is a giant community where people feel comfortable opening their door to strangers because in a way everyone knows everybody else—at least through one or two others. And this is one of many examples; hundreds or even thousands of reputation-based businesses and services like this are still being explored. Maybe you will pioneer the next?

Of course, none of this is adequate without putting in the work—reputation alone doesn't replace old-fashioned hustle. But sweat and effort will, if anything, be recognized *more* in the Reputation Economy. Take musical artist Greg Michael Gillis as an example. He began a musical career while studying biomedical engineering at Case Western Reserve University—one of the leading engineering schools in the country. After a few failed projects, he launched a solo career under the stage name Girl Talk and soon earned a reputation as one of the pioneers of the "mashup" style of music—the term for mixing samples from tens or hundreds of other sources to create an album that layers together sources as disparate as James Taylor singing over beats by Ludacris.[1] But Gillis didn't stop releasing a few albums; he quit his job as an engineer and began touring relentlessly, spending hundreds of days on the road every year creating his own immersive stage shows (balloons, confetti cannons, toilet paper, and always Gillis front and center dancing so hard that he ended up sweating through his trademark headband). Of the hundreds of people who have released mashup albums, Girl Talk is one of only two to be a "notable" artist in the genre, according to Wikipedia,[2] and is the only artist with two albums in the top ten mashups albums of all time according to *Vibe* magazine (#1 and #4, as it happens).[3] Gillis undoubtedly has immense imagination and musical talent, but he stands out from the crowd because he has also spent extraordinary effort in the studio and on the road building his own brand and evangelizing his new form of music.

Gillis is just one of many examples in this book that have focused on new economic opportunities brought by the Reputation Economy. But nothing limits these techniques to for-profit business. Of course, not everyone is interested in starting a business or making a profit—and the Reputation Economy will have just as many opportunities for those interested in bartering for fun and unique experiences without ever paying a dime.

The point is not that these particular services are the most fun or the most profitable (though many are both)—it's that the Reputation Economy is opening up a new model for collaboration. Of course, many services today rely on some measure of trust and security. Think of a hotel: in its simplest form, a brand name (whether it's a Quality Inn, a Motel 6, or a Four Seasons) tells visitors, "We have hundreds of rooms that meet a certain quality and safety standard." That standard varies by brand, but you know that you can travel to nearly any city, find the nearest Holiday Inn, and get the same quality (for better or for worse) there as at any other Holiday Inn anywhere else in the world. But services like Airbnb offer effectively the same security for both renter and rentee, without the big corporation or brand name in the middle: in fact, search for a room on a site like Airbnb and you can get even more information than you'd ever find on the Holiday Inn website, from photos to reviews to renter histories. And as the system grows, so do the number and depth of reviews, resulting in even better information for both parties and a more efficient matching between the two.

But again, the implications of this go well beyond finding a great vacation accommodation or building a peer-to-peer website. Do you have (or deserve) a good reputation in a narrow field? In today's Reputation Economy anyone can be the pioneer who builds a business or career around nearly anything that is currently being provided through an intermediary. Think about even a field like law. In the era prior to the Reputation Economy, it was nearly impossible for a prospective client to find the reputation of a lawyer if he or she wasn't already famous (think Johnnie Cochran). To fill the gap, law firms not only had to step in as intermediaries to guarantee a certain minimum quality but also had to find creative ways to develop their own reputations. But in a world where any potential client looking to hire a litigator can get a quick snapshot of his or her reputation on everything from cases won to billing practices to courtroom demeanor, lawyers no longer have to rely on the good name of their firm for their livelihood; they need to worry about only their own individual reputation.

It is in this way that the Reputation Economy has made it easier for *anyone* to hang a shingle outside the door and start his or her own business—whether as a litigator, an oil painting instructor, a CEO of a peer-to-peer apartment-sharing service, or anything else. In fact, in the Reputation Economy, essentially any third-party middleman can be cut out of the picture. So to seize these opportunities, figure out where your potential is being held back by traditional gatekeepers and aggregators. Then go directly to your market—by cutting out the middlemen.

The process will vary depending on your field or profession, but we can guarantee that there are fields nobody has even thought about yet that are subject to disaggregation and disintermediation through reputation. Find the ones that are best for you, and prosper by aggressively building your own reputation and then parlaying it into new business opportunities. Here are some general tips.

Be Proactive with Others

Of course, the ease with which anyone can start up a car-sharing service or a law practice will make it easier for you to strike out on your own when the time comes. Of course, this comes with drawbacks too; it means that as the Reputation Economy grows, more and more competitors will crop up as others come to the same realization you did. So how do you separate yourself from the chaff and ensure that when people search for "French language tutor" or "best graphics design instructor," it's your name that pops up? The simplest way is to simply encourage happy people to report your business (on sites like Angie's List or whatever's appropriate to your field) or professional successes (on general sites like LinkedIn or on specialized review sites for your field). The West Coast furniture company Living Spaces, for example, does this exceptionally well, especially for not being a massive corporation or heavily invested in social media. Like thousands of other businesses, it asks customers to routinely complete feedback surveys after purchase and delivery of furniture;

then it uses the feedback to improve its service, like thousands of other businesses. But Living Spaces has added a unique catch: if a consumer gives good ratings in the Living Spaces survey, then the survey software automatically gives the customer an extra coupon for a later purchase and asks if the customer would like to leave a review on the review site Yelp. Our own view is that exchanging value such as coupons for reviews may not be the best idea, but many businesses in many sectors of the economy have done so for decades, whether in exchange for reviews or for other forms of feedback, such as completion of surveys.

The strategy is brilliant in multiple ways. First, it encourages happy customers to leave reviews, combating a problem that many businesses face, namely that often only dissatisfied customers work up the energy to leave reviews, resulting in skewed reviews for businesses that have generally satisfied customers. Second, coupons encourage repeat business—this is the oldest marketing trick in the book. But finally and perhaps most brilliantly, by giving customers a coupon *before* asking them to review the company, the company has engendered goodwill—and plugged into the norm of reciprocity. Endless scientific studies suggest that people who receive a gift feel the need to reciprocate—don't take science's word, just look at the Hare Krishnas who give flowers to passersby before asking for donations, or organizations soliciting money that send a nickel to thousands of people, in the hopes that sending a nickel will return on investment in the form of dollars (seems wasteful to us, but the persistence of the strategy suggests that it works). In the case of Living Spaces, customers who receive the coupon will feel a need to reciprocate and will be apt to be even more positive about the company—and more likely to review. (Importantly, nothing about this process violates Yelp's endorsement guidelines as of this writing; nobody is being paid for a review directly.)

Be Unique

At the end of the day, however, you will stand out the most—and in the most positive way—if you offer something that is unique and personal to you. This is true no matter whether you're a business owner or manager, a working professional, a freelancer, or just someone trying to get ahead in your personal life. Being *you* will always help you succeed more than trying to conform to somebody else's mold. After all, one of the big benefits of the Reputation Economy is that the world will be able to judge you for who you are—rather than how well you fit into somebody else's predefined box. Take an example—pretend you're the world's best yo-yo–twirling clown. In the era before the Reputation Economy, your market was local and there was no way to find other people who were interested in both yo-yos and clowns at the same time. It's an admittedly small group, and the odds are good that you would be forced into just yo-yos or just clowning. But in the Reputation Economy you can find other people who are interested in both, no matter where they may be. In other words, while the Reputation Economy may have increased your competition for yo-yoing clowns, it also has broadened your market. It allows you to build a reputation, and maybe even a career, around skills that are uniquely you rather than having to pick from a list of more narrowly circumscribed options.

You probably aren't actually a yo-yo–twirling clown (call us if you are), but the same principle applies to nearly any unique combination of skills, talents, interests, and traits. Somewhere out there, somebody is looking for exactly the skills *you* have. Instead of trying to change yourself to fit what you think somebody else might want, embrace yourself and promote those unique things that only you can offer.

Earn It

We're in a new world of reputation, where reputations are made and lost in an instant, where everything you do will be tracked, calculated, measured, and analyzed, and where anyone can find out nearly everything about everyone else with just a click. And while there are plenty of things you can do to influence the conversation and shape public perceptions, at the end of the day the best reputation management strategy is simply to earn it by bringing more value to your employer and your customers, treating others well, and being socially and environmentally responsible. If you embrace the Reputation Economy, make sure you advertise your unique skills and talents, generate enough fodder for those reputation engines we keep talking about, and carefully curate the reputation you have.

Acknowledgments

We would like to thank Talia Krohn, our editor, who has been smart, deliberate, and indefatigable. We would like to thank all the terrific entrepreneurial teams that are helping make the Reputation Economy a reality. And we would like to thank our colleagues and friends for supporting the extra time required to make this book possible.

Notes

1. Welcome to the Reputation Economy

1. Sarah McBride, "Venture Capital Sees Big Returns on Big Data," *Huffington Post*, February 23, 2012, http://www.huffingtonpost.com/2012/02/23/venture-capital-sees-big-returns-on-big-data_n_1296519.html.

2. Jordan Novet, "Big Data Startups Pull in Big Money in 2013," *Venture Beat*, December 9, 2013, http://venturebeat.com/2013/12/09/big-data-startups-pull-in-big-money-in-2013/.

3. http://www.risk2reputation.com/files/Managing_Risks_to_Reputation_From_Theory_to_Practice.pdf@2. See also http://www.eiu.com/report_dl.asp?mode=fi&fi=1552294140.PDF@22.

4. Cory Doctorow, *Down and Out in the Magic Kingdom* (New York: St. Martin's Press, 2003), 14. The idea of a real-time view of somebody's reputation is not that far off; a smartphone can check Facebook instantly, and smartphone apps allow instant lookups of criminal histories for just a couple of dollars.

5. Ric Romero, "Are Insurance Companies Spying on Your Facebook Page?," ABC7, November 7, 2011, http://abclocal.go.com/kabc/story?section=news/consumer&id=8422388.

6. Leslie Scism and Mark Maremont, "Insurers Test Data Profiles to Identify Risky Clients," *Wall Street Journal*, November 19, 2010, http://online.wsj.com/article/SB10001424052748704648604575620750998072986.html?mod=googlenews_wsj.

7. Laura Mazzuca Toops, "Redlining Is Back—on the Web," *Property Casualty 360°*, February 9, 2012, http://www.propertycasualty360.com/2012/02/09/redlining-is-back—on-the-web?ref=hp.

8. American Express explained to one cardholder that his credit line was reduced because "our credit experience with customers who have made purchases at establishments where you have recently used your card" suggested that he too was a poor credit risk. Mike Stuckey, "AmEx Rates

Credit Risk by Where You Live, Shop," MSNBC, July 10, 2008, updated October 7, 2008, http://www.msnbc.msn.com/id/27055285/ns/business -stocks_and_economy/t/amex-rates-credit-risk-where-you-live-shop/# .T3lTMDEgeQA.

9. Lori Andrews, "Facebook Is Using You," *New York Times,* February 4, 2012, http://www.nytimes.com/2012/02/05/opinion/sunday/ facebook-is-using-you.html?_r=1&pagewanted=all.

10. Emily Steel, "Using Credit Cards to Target Web Ads," *Wall Street Journal,* October 25, 2011, http://online.wsj.com/article/ SB10001424052970204002304576627030651339352.html.

11. At present, it is limited to basic demographic data, but the "sky" in Las Vegas already records photos of players matched to their frequent player cards; it would be a trivial update to personalize the data and to record who went to what sections of the casino at what time. Shan Li and David Sarno, "Advertisers Start Using Facial Recognition to Tailor Pitches," *Los Angeles Times,* August 21, 2011, http://articles.latimes.com/2011/aug/21/business/la -fi-facial-recognition-20110821. David Thompson, coauthor of this book, is quoted in this article.

12. This has already happened. Scism and Maremont, "Insurers Test Data Profiles."

13. In *IMS Health v. Sorrell* (2011), the Supreme Court, by a vote of 6–3, went so far as to strike down a Vermont law that tried to regulate data brokers' access to prescription drug records on the basis of patient privacy. The Court ruled that even data brokers have free-speech rights.

2. Stored

1. "IBM Card Storage," photo, 1959, *Wikipedia,* https://en.wikipedia .org/wiki/File:IBM_card_storage.NARA.jpg.

2. Ryan Lawler, "Netflix Moves into the Cloud with Amazon Web Services," *Gigaom,* May 7, 2010, http://gigaom.com/2010/05/07/netflix -moves-into-the-cloud-with-amazon-web-services/.

3. Lucas Mearian, "Scientists Calculate Total Data Stored to Date: 295+ Exabytes," *Computerworld,* February 14, 2011, http://www .computerworld.com/s/article/9209158/Scientists_calculate_total_data _stored_to_date_295_exabytes.

4. Jon Stewart, "Global Data Storage Calculated at 295 Exabytes," BBC News, February 11, 2011, http://www.bbc.co.uk/news/technology-12419672.

5. A 6.25-terabyte tape cartridge is available at TapeResources.com for $110, http://www.taperesources.com/FJ-LTO-6.html.

6. Todd Bishop, "Microsoft Offers More Storage on Free Hotmail," *Seattle Post-Intelligencer,* June 23, 2004, http://www.seattlepi.com/business/ article/Microsoft-offers-more-storage-on-free-Hotmail-1147847.php.

7. Rob Waugh, " 'Deleted' Facebook Photos Still Viewable Three Years Later," *Daily Mail,* February 6, 2012, http://www.dailymail.co.uk/sciencetech/article-2097005/Deleted-Facebook-photos-online-years -later—company-STILL-wont-fix-fault-systems.html.

8. David G. Savage, "Parents Cleared of False Allegations Remain on State's Child Abuser List," *Los Angeles Times,* February 23, 2010, http://www .latimes.com/news/local/la-me-court-registration23-2010feb23,0,5147585 .story.

9. Will Reisman, "Muni Expanding Camera Program to Nab Drivers in Transit-Only Lanes," *San Francisco Examiner,* February 10, 2012, http:// www.sfexaminer.com/sanfrancisco/muni-expanding-camera-program-to -nab-drivers-in-transit-only-lanes/Content?oid=2194760.

10. National Vehicle Locator, http://ddq74coujkv1i.cloudfront.net/ _misc/PDFs/National-Veh-Locator.pdf.

11. Artem Yankov, "How to Find Facebook Users on Match.com by Using Face Recognition Tools," *Experimental Coding,* February 26, 2014, http://artemyankov.com/post/18307807152/how-to-find-facebook-users-on -match-com-by-using-face.

12. Stephanie Clifford and Jessica Silver-Greenberg, "Business Retailers Use Databases to Track Worker Thefts," *New York Times,* April 2, 2013, http://www.nytimes.com/2013/04/03/business/retailers-use-databases-to -track-worker-thefts.html?pagewanted=all&_r=2&.

3. Scored

1. Jeffrey Dean and Sanjay Ghemawat, "MapReduce: Simplified Data Processing on Large Clusters," USENIX Association, https://www.usenix .org/legacy/event/osdi04/tech/full_papers/dean/dean.pdf.

2. http://www.infoq.com/interviews/wiggins-heroku-ec2-cloud.

3. http://www.computerworld.com/s/article/9209158/Scientists _calculate_total_data_stored_to_date_295_exabytes.

4. http://www.bbc.co.uk/news/technology-12419672.

5. https://www.facebook.com/note.php?note_id=16121578919.

6. http://www.seattlepi.com/business/article/Microsoft-offers-more -storage-on-free-Hotmail-1147847.php.

7. "Apache Hadoop," *Wikipedia,* http://en.wikipedia.org/w/index.php?title =Apache_Hadoop&oldid=552614060#Facebook (accessed April 7, 2014).

8. Charles Babcock, "Yahoo and Hadoop: In It for the Long Term," *InformationWeek,* June 15, 2012, http://www.informationweek.com/ development/database/yahoo-and-hadoop-in-it-for-the-long-term/240002133.

9. "Six Super-scale Hadoop Deployments," *Datanami,* April 26, 2012, http://www.datanami.com/datanami/2012-04-26/six_super-scale_hadoop _deployments.html, 2.

10. Derrick Harris, "10 Ways Companies Are Using Hadoop for More Than Ads," *Gigaom,* June 5, 2012, http://gigaom.com/2012/06/05/10-ways -companies-are-using-hadoop-to-do-more-than-serve-ads/.

11. "Six Super-scale Hadoop Deployments," 7.

12. Craig Allen, "Data Supplements: How Much Should You Gather on Your Customers?," Delphi Analytics, April 17, 2013, http://www.delphianalytics .net/data-supplements-how-much-should-you-gather-on-your-customers/.

13. Tim Gruber, "Electronic Scores Rank Consumers by Potential Value," *New York Times,* August 18, 2012, http://www.nytimes.com/2012/ 08/19/business/electronic-scores-rank-consumers-by-potential-value .html?ref=natashasinger.

14. eBureau, "eScore's," data sheet, http://www.eureau.com/sites/ default/files/file/datasheets/ebureau_escore_datasheet.pdf.

15. "Very Personal Finance," *Economist,* June 2, 2012, http://www .economist.com/node/21556263.

16. Joseph Walker, "Data Mining to Recruit Sick People," *Wall Street Journal,* December 17, 2013, http://online.wsj.com/news/articles/ SB10001424052702303722104579240140554518458.

17. Lyneka Little, "Court Okays Facebook Party Photos in Workers Comp Claim," ABC News, February 3, 2012, http://abcnews.go.com/blogs/business/ 2012/02/court-okays-facebook-party-photos-in-workers-comp-claim/.

18. Joan E. Collier, "California Woman Found Guilty of Workers' Compensation Fraud," Workers' Compensation Institute, May 9, 2012, http://www.wci360.com/news/article/california-woman-found-guilty-of -workers-compensation-fraud#.UYTAPbV8nng.

19. "Very Personal Finance."

20. Kate Freeman, "Klout Ranks the Time 100: Guess Who's #1?," *Mashable,* April 20, 2012, http://mashable.com/2012/04/20/klout-time -magazine-100/.

21. Nicholas A. Christakis and James H. Fowler, "The Spread of Obesity in a Large Social Network over 32 Years," *New England Journal of Medicine* 357, no. 4 (2007): 370–79.

22. "Facebook Abstainers Could Be Labeled Suspicious," *Slashdot,* n.d., http://tech.slashdot.org/story/12/07/29/1627203/facebook-abstainers-could -be-labeled-suspicious (accessed April 7, 2014).

4. Potent

1. "Faithfully," by Arnel Pineda with the Zoo Band, uploaded to YouTube July 26, 2008, http://www.youtube.com/watch?v=ragdoUO6s5w (14—/ 979+ as of last review).

2. "A Journey Back," CBS News, June 1, 2008, http://www.cbsnews .com/8301-3445_162-4142967.html.

3. "Cheapest Audition Ever: Journey Searches YouTube, Finds New Lead Singer," *Stereogum*, December 6, 2007, http://stereogum.com/7402/cheapest_audition_ever_journey_searches_youtube_fi/video/.

4. "A Journey Back," CBS News.

5. "Mars One," *Wikipedia*, http://en.wikipedia.org/wiki/Mars_One (accessed April 7, 2014).

6. Alison Doyle, "The Number of Job Applications per Opening," About.com, August 18, 2013, http://jobsearch.about.com/b/2013/08/18/the-number-of-job-applications-per-opening.htm.

7. "Are Emily and Greg More Employable Than Lakisha and Jamal? A Field Experiment on Labor Market Discrimination," *American Economic Review* 94 (2004): 991, 992, http://www2.econ.iastate.edu/classes/econ321/orazem/bertrand_emily.pdf.

8. Their website is http://images.google.com/.

5. Discoverable

1. See, e.g., Andy Warhol, "Illustration of Shoe and Belt," *McCall's*, October 1953, uploaded to Flickr, December 6, 2008, http://www.flickr.com/photos/23097960@N04/3087751263/in/photostream/.

2. We can say this with confidence because the range of variability is so large among first job performances; sometimes it becomes clear within the first week that a candidate qualified on paper just can't hack it in real life.

3. See the segment on Sam Lassin in John Tozzi, Stacy Perman, and Nick Leiber, "2009 Finalists: America's Best Entrepreneurs," *Businessweek*, October 6, 2009, http://images.businessweek.com/ss/09/10/1009_entrepreneurs_25_and_under/7.htm.

4. Among many, Don Moore, "Stop Being Deceived by Interviews When You're Hiring," *Forbes*, February 7, 2012, http://www.forbes.com/sites/forbesleadershipforum/2012/02/07/stop-being-deceived-by-interviews-when-youre-hiring/.

5. Kevin Bonsor, "How the NFL Draft Works," *How Stuff Works*, n.d., http://entertainment.howstuffworks.com/nfl-draft4.htm.

6. Pamela Hawley, "How to Save Yourself the High Cost of a Wrong Hire," *Fast Company*, May 9, 2012, http://www.fastcompany.com/1836623/how-save-yourself-high-cost-wrong-hire.

7. "The ROI of Background Screening: Making Financial Success of 'Best Practices,'" *HR Management Magazine*, https://www.e-verifile.com/doc/eFYI-ARTICLE-HRMgt-ROIofBckgrdScreening.pdf.

8. "Court Okays Barring High IQs for Cops," ABC News, September 8, 2000, http://abcnews.go.com/US/court-oks-barring-high-iqs-cops/story?id=95836.

9. M. J. Fry, Andrew W. Lundberg, and Jeffrey W. Ohlmann, "A Player

Selection Heuristic for a Sports League Draft," *Journal of Quantitative Analysis in Sports* 3, no. 2 (2007), http://people.emich.edu/aross15/math319/player-selection-heuristic-sports-league-draft.pdf.

6. Disruptive

1. https://nces.ed.gov/programs/digest/d12/tables/dt12_236.asp.

2. "China Has 25 Million College Students," Xinhua, October 18, 2007, http://www.china.org.cn/english/China/228657.htm.

3. U.S Census Bureau, *Number Enrolled in College by Type of School and Enrollment Status, 1970–2011,* http://www.census.gov/hhes/school/data/cps/historical/TableA-7.pdf.

4. "Tuition Inflation," *FinAid,* 2014, http://www.finaid.org/savings/tuition-inflation.phtml.

5. National Center for Educational Statistics, *Digest of Education Statistics, 2011,* NCES 2012001 (Washington, DC, 2012), 532 and subsequent charts.

6. Richard Arum and Josipa Roksa, "Are Undergraduates Actually Learning Anything?," *Chronicle of Higher Education,* January 18, 2011, http://chronicle.com/article/Are-Undergraduates-Actually/125979/.

7. Derek Bok, *Our UnderAchieving Colleges: A Candid Look at How Much Students Learn and Why They Should Be Learning More* (Princeton, NJ: Princeton University Press, 2006).

8. See Derek Bok, "Are Colleges Failing? Higher Ed Needs New Lesson Plans," *Boston Globe,* December 18, 2005, http://www.boston.com/news/education/higher/articles/2005/12/18/are_colleges_failing/?page=full.

9. University of Texas at Austin, "Budget 101: How the Money Gets Used," last updated May 16, 2011, http://www.utexas.edu/finances/money-used.html.

10. Ohio State University, "Statistical Summary," 2013, http://www.osu.edu/osutoday/stuinfo.php.

11. W. Craig Riddell, "Understanding 'Sheepskin Effects' in the Returns to Education," Paper for presentation at the CLSRN Workshop, University of Toronto, November 18–19, 2008, http://www.clsrn.econ.ubc.ca/hrsdc/papers/Paper%20no.%202%20-%20Craig%20Riddell%20-%20Sheepskin%20Effects.pdf.

12. Bryan Caplan, "The Present Value of a Sheepskin," Library of Economics and Liberty, http://econlog.econlib.org/archives/2012/01/the_present_val.html.

13. For example, "Validity," *Assessment Decision Guide,* U.S. Office of Personnel Management, http://apps.opm.gov/ADT/Content.aspx?page=2-02&JScript=1.

14. Vikrant Soman and Anmol Madan, "Social Signaling: Predicting the Outcome of Job Interviews from Vocal Tone and Prosody," http://web .media.mit.edu/~anmol/ICASSP_interviews_v12.pdf.

15. Alison Doyle, "The Number of Job Applications Per Opening," Job Searching, About.com, http://jobsearch.about.com/b/2013/08/18/the -number-of-job-applications-per-opening.htm.

16. For example, Boston College's law school allows employers to select 75 percent of their interview candidates, but requires employers to take 25 percent through a preference lottery: http://www.bc.edu/schools/law/ services/career/employers/oncampusinterviews.html.

17. Posting on *Gadball,* http://www.gadball.com/job/26306262/ research-and-operations-s/.

18. Salary: divide $1 million by number of years. David A. Kaplan, "Bill Gates' Favorite Teacher," *CNN Money,* August 24, 2010. http://money.cnn .com/2010/08/23/technology/sal_khan_academy.fortune/index.htm.

19. Tom Wolfe, "Greenwich Time," *New York Times,* September 27, 2008, http://www.nytimes.com/2008/09/28/opinion/28wolfe.html?_r=0.

20. Khan Academy website, https://www.khanacademy.org/about.

21. Kaplan, "Bill Gates' Favorite Teacher."

22. "Khan Academy Founder Proposes a New Type of College," *Chronicle of Higher Education,* November 29, 2012, http://chronicle.com/ blogs/wiredcampus/khan-academy-founder-proposes-a-new-type-of -college/41160.

23. At the time, any mail would have been delivered by the then-new English postal service. "Getting the Word Out: Franklin's Communications Revolutions," The E Pluribus Unum Project, Assumption College, http:// www1.assumption.edu/ahc/1770s/pcomcircuit.html.

24. Salman Khan, "My View: The Future of Credentials," CNN.com, October 4, 2012, http://schoolsofthought.blogs.cnn.com/2012/10/04/my -view-the-future-of-credentials/.

25. VORP is calculated by the number of additional runs per season or wins per season a player will provide above the level of the top minor league or "waiver wire" player available to replace him. It is one of the core statistics of Sabermetrics, the system made famous by the movie *Moneyball.*

26. Jackie MacMullan, "Burning Desire," *Boston Globe,* October 7, 2009, http://www.boston.com/sports/baseball/redsox/articles/2009/10/07/ red_sox_youkilis_has_burning_desire/?page=full.

27. "Lifetime Earnings: College Graduates Still Earn More," National Association of College and University Business Officers, October 18, 2012, http://www.nacubo.org/Research/Research_News/Lifetime_Earnings _College_Graduates_Still_Earn_More.html.

28. Glen Tickle, "The Story Behind This Robotic Butt," *Geekosystem,* November 12, 2013, http://www.geekosystem.com/robot-butt-simulator/.

7. Instant

1. Project Glass video on YouTube, http://www.youtube.com/watch?v=9c6W4CCU9M4.

2. Anna Breslaw, "New STD-Free Certification App Invented for the Youngs," *Jezebel,* December 26, 2012, http://jezebel.com/5971182/new-std+free-certification-app-invented-for-the-youngs.

3. Seth Porges, "Read These Tips, or Nobody Will Ever Let You Be an Airbnb Guest Again," *Gizmodo,* June 14, 2012, http://gizmodo.com/5918204/read-these-tips-or-nobody-will-ever-let-you-be-an-airbnb-guest-again.

4. Beth Spotswood, "Tourist Trapped: Getting Dumped by OpenTable.com," *SFGate,* September 19, 2011, blog.sfgate.com/culture/2011/09/19/tourist-trapped-getting-dumped-by-opentable-com.

5. Gregory Ferenstein, "Facedeals: Check-In on Facebook with Facial Recognition. Creepy or Awesome?," *TechCrunch,* August 10, 2012, http://techcrunch.com/2012/08/10/facedeals-check-in-on-facebook-with-facial-recognition-creepy-or-awesome/.

6. Kashmir Hill, "How Target Figured Out a Teen Girl Was Pregnant Before Her Father Did," *Forbes,* February 16, 2012, http://www.forbes.com/sites/kashmirhill/2012/02/16/how-target-figured-out-a-teen-girl-was-pregnant-before-her-father-did/.

7. Edward Stringham, "Ex Ante Risk Management by Paypal and Other Intermediaries: How Technologically Advanced Markets Can Work Even When Fraud Is 'Legal,'" http://econ.as.nyu.edu/docs/IO/26327/Stringham_09172012.pdf.

8. Cash America 2011 Form 10-K, p. 53, http://www.cashamerica.com/Files/Annual%20reports/Cash%20America%202011%20Annual%20Report.pdf.

9. Mark Flannery and Katherine Samolyk, "Pay Lending: Do the Costs Justify the Price?," working paper, FDIC Center for Financial Research, June 2005, p. 16, http://www.fdic.gov/bank/analytical/cfr/2005/wp2005/cfrwp_2005-09_flannery_samolyk.pdf.

10. Tim Lewis, "With Wonga, Your Prosperity Could Count on an Algorithm," *Guardian,* October 15, 2011, http://www.guardian.co.uk/money/2011/oct/16/wonga-algorithm-lending-debt-data.

11. Mary Elizabeth Williams, "What Really Happened to Sunil Tripathi?," *Salon,* April 24, 2013, http://www.salon.com/2013/04/24/what_really_happened_to_sunil_tripathi/.

8. Portable

1. Studies exist to show that the ability to squat large weights is correlated with faster sprinting speed, which is crucial for performance in many sports. See, for example, Jeffrey M. McBride et al., "Relationship

Between Maximal Squat Strength and Five, Ten, and Forty Yard Sprint Times," *Journal of Strength and Conditioning Research*, September 2009, http://libres.uncg.edu/ir/asu/f/Triplett_Travis_2009_Relationship _Between_Maximal.pdf.

2. Cindy Zhan, "The Correlation Between Music and Math: A Neurobiology Perspective," *Serendip*, January 16, 2008, http://serendip .brynmawr.edu/exchange/node/1869.

3. David B. Gross and Nicholas S. Souleles, "An Empirical Analysis of Personal Bankruptcy and Delinquency," *Review of Financial Studies*, Spring 2002, note 1, http://finance.wharton.upenn.edu/~souleles/research/papers/ Default_RFSversion.pdf.

4. Scott Fay, Erik Hurst, and Michelle J. White, "The Household Bankruptcy Decision," *American Economic Review*, June 2002, 706–718, http://scholar.google.com/scholar?cluster=6640412969679321777&hl =en&as_sdt=0,5&as_vis=1 (page 8, citing Visa 1997).

5. http://faculty.chicagobooth.edu/workshops/finance/archive/pdf/ negative_eq_july.pdf.

9. Inaccurate

1. See Michael Fertick and David Thompson, *Wild West 2.0: How to Protect and Restore Your Reputation on the Untamed Social Frontier* (New York: AMACOM, 2010), pp. 56–57.

2. For example: https://twitter.com/TMnY/status/226619997953331200.

3. Salvador Rodriguez, "Swedish Firm's Apple Hoax Shows Gullibility of Online Readers," *Los Angeles Times*, August 14, 2012, http://articles .latimes.com/2012/aug/14/business/la-fi-tn-apple-hoax-20120814.

4. Curt Finch, "The Klout Score, a Way to Measure Online Influence," *Inc.com*, January 21, 2011, http://www.inc.com/tech-blog/the-klout-score-a -way-to-measure-online-influence.html; Jay Baer, "Solving Klout's 'Warren Buffett Problem,'" Convince and Convert, March 29, 2013, http://www .convinceandconvert.com/social-pros-podcast/solving-klouts-warren -buffett-problem/.

5. "Berkshire Hathaway Annual Meeting Keeps Growing," *Bloomberg Businessweek*, May 4, 2013, http://www.businessweek.com/ap/2013-05-04/ berkshire-hathaway-annual-meeting-keeps-growing.

6. https://twitter.com/LesleyHauler.

7. http://klout.com/LesleyHauler.

8. Adriaan Pelzer, "Klout Is Broken," RAAK, December 2, 2010, http://wewillraakyou.com/2010/12/klout-is-broken.

9. http://www.neilkodner.com/2010/12/my-twitter-bots-tens-of -thousands-of-followers-cant-be-wrong/.

10. http://cs.nyu.edu/trackmenot/#version.

11.　Reuven Cohen, "Dept. of Homeland Security Forced to Release List of Keywords Used to Monitor Social Networking Sites," *Forbes*, May 26, 2012, http://www.forbes.com/sites/reuvencohen/2012/05/26/department-of-homeland-security-forced-to-release-list-of-keywords-used-to-monitor-social-networking-sites/2/.

12.　As of writing, available at domains such as xina.114.at/lock4494.html.

13.　Josh Constine, "BuzzFeed's First Acquisition Kingfish Labs Could Make Its FB Ads Go More Viral Than Football Cats," *TechCrunch*, September 13, 2012, http://techcrunch.com/2012/09/13/buzzfeed-kingfish-labs.

14.　Eric Eldon, "TheComplete.me Launches Social Dating Site, Matches with $1.22M from Industry Leaders," *TechCrunch*, April 16, 2012, http://techcrunch.com/2012/04/16/thecomplete-me-launches-social-dating-site-matches-with-1-22m-from-industry-leaders.

10. Proactive

1.　Sid Kirchheimer, "Where's Teddy Now?," *South Florida Sun-Sentinel*, April 22, 1987, http://articles.sun-sentinel.com/1987-04-22/features/8701250837_1_teddy-ruxpin-toy-store-toy-chest.

2.　Don Southerton, "Part 2—Hyundai, the Excel, and the 1986 U.S. Launch," *Bridging Culture Worldwide*, April 28, 2012, http://bridgingculturekorea.blogspot.com/2012/04/hyundai-excel-and-1986-us-launch.html.

3.　"Glengarry Glen Ross (film)," *Wikiquote*, http://en.wikiquote.org/wiki/Glengarry_Glen_Ross_(film).

4.　Bill Vlasic and Bradley A. Stertz, *Taken for a Ride: How Daimler-Benz Drove Off with Chrysler* (New York: William Morrow, 2000), excerpt at http://www.businessweek.com/2000/00_23/b3684147.htm.

5.　"U.S. Automobile Production Figures," *Wikipedia*, http://en.wikipedia.org/wiki/U.S._Automobile_Production_Figures.

6.　Robyn Meredith, "Sales by Ford Aid a Strong September for Auto Makers," *New York Times*, October 4, 1996, http://www.nytimes.com/1996/10/04/business/sales-by-ford-aid-a-strong-september-for-auto-makers.html; Robyn Meredith, "Auto Makers Fell Shy of Expectations," *New York Times*, November 6, 1996, http://www.nytimes.com/1996/11/06/business/auto-makers-fell-shy-of-expectations.html.

7.　Michelle Krebs, "To Counter Stigma, Hyundai Bolsters Warranty," *New York Times*, November 8, 1998, http://www.nytimes.com/1998/11/08/automobiles/to-counter-stigma-hyundai-bolsters-warranty.html.

8.　Tom Krisher, "How Hyundai Went from Joke to Contender in US," *Arizona Republic*, April 12, 2012, http://www.azcentral.com/

arizonarepublic/business/articles/20120412how-hyundai-went-from-joke
-contender-us.html.

9. Krebs, "To Counter Stigma, Hyundai Bolsters Warranty."

10. Greg Anderson, "Sonata Great Car, But Sonata Bad Car," Edmunds
.com, January 1, 1999, http://www.edmunds.com/hyundai/sonata/1999/
road-test.html.

11. Dave Boe, "Hyundai Announces New 10-Year Warranty
Program," *Chicago Daily Herald,* November 9, 1998, http://nl.newsbank
.com/nl-search/we/Archives?p_product=ADHB&p_theme=adhb&p
_action=search&p_maxdocs=200&p_topdoc=1&p_text_direct-0
=0ED028F5D5CF884B&p_field_direct-0=document_id&p_perpage
=10&p_sort=YMD_date:D&s_trackval=GooglePM.

12. See article at http://news.google.com/newspapers?id
=iRgiAAAAIBAJ&sjid=MaYFAAAAIBAJ&pg=4931,5947705&dq
=hyundai+warranty&hl=en.

13. Andrew Peterson, "Hyundai, Kia Set New Records in 2010 with
Sales of 538,228 and 356,268 Vehicles Respectively," *Motor Trend,* January 4,
2011, http://wot.motortrend.com/hyundai-kia-set-new-records-2010-sales
-538228-356268-vehicles-respectively-21926.html#axzz2cgKi8NXY.

14. Timothy Cain, "2012 Year End United States Auto Sales Brand
Rankings," *Good Car Bad Car,* January 3, 2013, http://www.goodcarbadcar
.net/2013/01/2012-usa-auto-sales-brand-rankings.html.

15. Corky Siemaszko, "Yahoo! Honcha Marissa Mayer Outrages
Minions by Building Nursery Near Her Office After Barring Employess
Working from Home," *New York Daily News,* February 27, 2013, http://www
.nydailynews.com/news/national/yahoo-nurserygate-article-1.1275069.

16. Jon Swartz and Nancy Blair, "Analysis: Reported Tumblr Deal a
Bold Move for Yahoo," *USA Today,* May 19, 2013, http://www.usatoday
.com/story/tech/2013/05/19/yahoo-tumblr-analysis/2324455.

17. http://www.quora.com/Facebook-Engineering/What-is-Facebooks
-architecture.

18. "Orders of Magnitude (Power)," *Wikipedia,* http://en.wikipedia
.org/wiki/Orders_of_magnitude_(power)#megawatt_.28106_watts.29;
http://www.oregonlive.com/silicon-forest/index.ssf/2011/12/apple_eyes
_prineville_site_for.html.

19. http://gigaom.com/2012/08/17/a-rare-look-inside-facebooks
-oregon-data-center-photos-video/.

20. Ibid.

21. Veerendra Mulay, "Humidity Excursions in Facebook Prineville
Data Center," *Electronics Cooling,* December 10, 2012, http://www
.electronics-cooling.com/2012/12/humidity-excursions-in-facebook
-prineville-data-center.

22. "Don't Bet on Another's Game," *New York Times,*

November 10, 1901, http://query.nytimes.com/gst/abstract.html?res
=F60815FD3D5C15738DDDA90994D9415B818CF1D3.

23. Wayne F. Cascio, "The High Cost of Low Wages," *Harvard Business Review,* December 2006, http://hbr.org/2006/12/the-high-cost-of-low -wages/ar/1.

Conclusion: Be an Innovator

1. "Hold Up," from *Night Ripper* (Illegal Art, 2006).

2. "Mashup (music)," *Wikipedia,* http://en.wikipedia.org/w/index .php?title=Mashup_(music)&oldid=590328110.

3. http://www.vibe.com/photo-gallery/top-10-mashup-albums-all -time?page=11K.

Index

About the Author

MICHAEL FERTIK is the leading authority on digital reputation and privacy. He founded Reputation.com with the belief that people and businesses have the right to control and protect their online reputation and privacy. A futurist, Michael is credited with pioneering the field of online reputation management (ORM).

Michael was recently named Entrepreneur of the Year by TechAmerica, an annual award given by the technology industry trade group to an individual they feel embodies the entrepreneurial spirit that made the U.S. technology sector the world's leader.

He is a member of the World Economic Forum Agenda Council on the Future of the Internet and a recipient of the World Economic Forum Technology Pioneer 2011 Award, which named Reputation.com, through his leadership, a Global Growth Company in 2012. He is also a member of the Aspen CEO Roundtable.

The named inventor on multiple patents, Michael is also active in teaching, most recently through an appointment at Harvard Law School for Spring 2015.

Fertik is an industry commentator with guest columns for *Harvard Business Review,* Reuters, *Inc.com,* and *Newsweek.* Named a LinkedIn Influencer, he regularly blogs on current events as well as developments in entrepreneurship and technology. Fertik frequently appears on national and international television and radio, including the BBC, *Good Morning America*, *The Today Show*, *Dr. Phil*, *The Early Show*, CNN, Fox, Bloomberg, and MSNBC. He is the coauthor of a previous bestselling book, *Wild West 2.0*. He is also a published and prize-winning fiction author and short-film writer.

Fertik founded his first Internet company while at Harvard College. He received his JD from Harvard Law School. He lives in Palo Alto.